C ULTURE SMART!
VENEZUELA

Russell Maddicks

·K·U·P·E·R·A·R·D·

ISBN 978 1 85733 657 3
This book is also available as an e-book: eISBN 978 1 85733 661 0

British Library Cataloguing in Publication Data
A CIP catalogue entry for this book is available from the British Library

First published in Great Britain
by Kuperard, an imprint of Bravo Ltd
59 Hutton Grove, London N12 8DS
Tel: +44 (0) 20 8446 2440   Fax: +44 (0) 20 8446 2441
www.culturesmart.co.uk
Inquiries: sales@kuperard.co.uk

Distributed in the United States and Canada
by Random House Distribution Services
1745 Broadway, New York, NY 10019
Tel: +1 (212) 572-2844   Fax: +1 (212) 572-4961
Inquiries: csorders@randomhouse.com

Series Editor Geoffrey Chesler
Design Bobby Birchall

Printed in Malaysia

About the Author

RUSSELL MADDICKS is a BBC-trained journalist who lived in Venezuela for eleven years. He traveled the length and breadth of the country, and to finance his stay he worked in jobs that helped him to get under the skin of his adopted home: as an English teacher at the British Council; a jungle guide taking tour groups to the base of Angel Falls and the top of Roraima; a translator and interpreter; and a reporter on an English-language newspaper. There are few corners of Venezuela he hasn't visited in his quest to explore every facet of this fascinating country. He is the author of the *Bradt Guide to Venezuela* (2011).

The publishers would like to thank **CultureSmart!**Consulting for its help in researching and developing the concept for this series.

CultureSmart!Consulting creates tailor-made seminars and consultancy programs to meet a wide range of corporate, public-sector, and individual needs. Whether delivering courses on multicultural team building in the USA, preparing Chinese engineers for a posting in Europe, training call-center staff in India, or raising the awareness of police forces to the needs of diverse ethnic communities, it provides essential, practical, and powerful skills worldwide to an increasingly international workforce.

For details, visit www.culturesmartconsulting.com

CultureSmart!Consulting and **CultureSmart!** guides have both contributed to and featured regularly in the weekly travel program "Fast Track" on BBC World TV.

contents

contents

Map of Venezuela

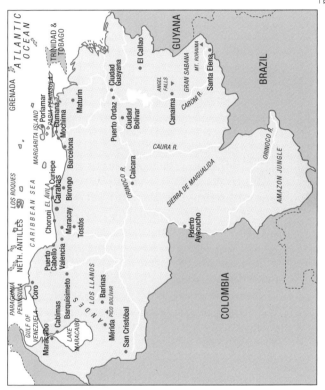

introduction

An influential oil producer with a charismatic president at its helm since 1999, Venezuela is a vast, sometimes frustrating, but never dull country. It is one of the most complex countries in Latin America, and one of the least understood.

Venezuela's extraordinary geographical diversity ranges from picture-postcard Caribbean beaches to pristine rain forests inhabited by jungle tribes, historic UNESCO World Heritage Sites, spectacular mountain treks, and the world's highest waterfall. Its unique culinary traditions, linguistic quirks, colorful history, and busy annual cycle of festivities are part of a rich cultural heritage left by the Spanish conquistadors and the slaves brought from Africa, combined with elements that can be traced back to the indigenous Amerindian inhabitants.

An ambitious attempt to benefit the poor and redistribute oil wealth by President Hugo Chávez has seen a major political transformation in recent years. This has put a severe strain on Venezuela's traditional ties with the USA, the destination of 60 percent of its oil exports. This move toward a socialist model inspired by the independence hero Simón Bolívar has seen new ties forged with like-minded countries in the region, such as Brazil, Bolivia, Cuba, and Argentina, and with non-traditional allies like Russia, China, and Iran.

But despite Chávez's steadfast attempts to confront his powerful northern neighbor and reduce Venezuela's economic dependence on the

United States, Miami remains the top holiday destination for Venezuelans traveling abroad, baseball beats soccer as the preferred sport, and teenage girls still cover their bedroom walls with posters of American idols like Justin Bieber.

Venezuelans are known for being friendly, gregarious, and outgoing. They value family above everything, and love to criticize the status quo—but they are also fiercely proud and protective of their homeland and react poorly to criticism from outsiders. They are optimistic and forward-looking, quick with a joke, and instantly familiar with strangers. The key to their confidence comes from the large extended family groups they grow up in, and the constant round of birthdays, baptisms, weddings, and holidays that bring them all together for music, dancing, and general merrymaking.

Culture Smart! Venezuela takes you beyond the stereotypical descriptions of a tropical petro-state, famous for its beauty queens and its populist president, to provide you with an insider's understanding of the country and its people. It looks at the historical roots of modern-day social values and attitudes. It offers advice on what to expect and how to build personal ties, and outlines how flexibility and patience are crucial to any business venture. Practical tips, valuable insights, and vital statistics have been marshaled to enable you to get to the heart of this vibrant, sometimes contradictory, and increasingly important country.

Key Facts

Official Name	Republica Bolivariana de Venezuela	(Bolivarian Republic of Venezuela)
Capital City	Caracas	Pop. 3.2 million. Altitude 2,985 feet (910 m)
Other Main Cities	Maracaibo, Valencia, Barquisimeto, Maracay, Ciudad Guyana	
Area	352,140 sq. miles (912,050 sq. km)	Sixth-largest country in South America
Geography	Northeast South America. Amazonas region is 1° north of the equator.	Borders Caribbean in north, Colombia in west, Guyana in east, and Brazil in south.
Terrain	Diverse. Andean mountains, Caribbean coast and islands, wetlands, tropical rain forests, savannas, deserts, lakes, major river systems, flat-topped *tepui* mountains. Longest coastline in Caribbean. Orinoco River and Delta	
Climate	Varies with altitude. Coast dry and hot, rain forest hot, wet, humid; Andes cool, temperate.	Caracas temperature varies from 90°F (32°C) high to 45°F (7°C) low.
Seasons	Dry and rainy seasons. Dry months Dec.–May. Rainy months June–Nov.	Proximity to Equator means that sunrise (about 5:30 a.m.) and sunset (about 6:00 p.m.) change little throughout year.
Population	Approx. 28 million	90% live in cities.
Life Expectancy	Men 70.84 Women 77.17	Infant mortality 1.7%

Ethnic Makeup	69% *mestizo* (mixed-race Amerindian, European, African); 20% European; 9% African; 2% Amerindian	
Language	Spanish; 28 indigenous languages	
Literacy Rate	98%	
Religion	90% Roman Catholic; 8% Protestant and Evangelical; 2% indigenous beliefs and other religions.	Protestant numbers have significantly increased in recent years.
System of Government	Democratic federal republic. Unicameral national assembly elected every 5 years. The president, elected every 6 years, is chief of state and head of government.	23 states, one Federal District (Caracas), and one Federal Dependency
Media	Privately owned national newspapers *El Nacional* and *El Universal*	
Currency	Bolivar Fuerte (currency code VEF). In plural, Bolívares Fuerte, or BsF	Divided into 100 céntimos.
Electricity	110 volts, 60 Hz	
Internet Domain	.ve	
Telephone	Venezuela's country code is 58.	Cities have their own codes (Caracas 0212).
Video/TV	NTSC. DVD Zone 4	
Time Zone	UTC/GMT -4:30 hours	

chapter one

LAND & PEOPLE

GEOGRAPHY

Occupying an area of 352,140 square miles
(912,050 sq. km), Venezuela is the sixth-largest
country in South America, covering a greater area
than either the US states of California, Oregon, and
Washington, or, in European terms, Spain, Portugal,
the UK, and Ireland, put together. It lies on the
northern coast of South America, wedged between
Colombia in the west, Guyana in the east, and Brazil
in the south. To the north it faces the Caribbean
and the Atlantic. It has the longest coastline in the
Caribbean, and a number of offshore islands,
including the tourist mecca of Margarita.

Located less than 1° north of the
equator, Venezuela is a tropical
country blessed with a number
of very different geographical
landscapes and microclimates,
including Andean mountains,
Amazonian rainforests, arid deserts,
seasonally flooded plains, coral
islands, the Orinoco River Delta,
the ancient rock formations of the
Guiana Shield, and the waterfall
with the longest drop in the world—
Salto Ángel (Angel Falls).

The south of the country is covered with hot, humid rain forests that are home to indigenous people, some of whom, such as the Yanomami, still live much as they did before the arrival of Columbus. Coursing through this heavily forested region is the Orinoco River, one of the longest rivers in South America. The Orinoco runs for 1,330 miles (2,140 km) from its source on the Cerro Delgado-Chalbaud in the Sierra Parima mountains on the Venezuela–Brazil border to the Delta Amacuro—home to Warao Indians living in houses on stilts—where it branches out into a hundred rivers and creeks before discharging its waters into the Atlantic Ocean. Another pristine river basin, which feeds into the massive Guri hydroelectric dam, is that of the Rio Caura, home to the Yekwana people.

In the Andean region of Mérida are high mountains and intermontane valleys known as *páramos*, where ruddy-faced farmers still use oxen to plow terraced fields. Overlooking the student city of Mérida are the country's highest peaks—Pico Bolívar at 16,341 feet (4,981 m) and Pico Humboldt at 16,207 feet (4,940 m)—which are joined by a permanent, if shrinking, glacier. Popular with hikers and adventure sports enthusiasts, the Andes also attract wildlife watchers seeking the unusual cock of the rock and the rare spectacled bear.

The largest lake in South America, and the source of much of Venezuela's oil wealth, the brackish Lake Maracaibo is fed by freshwater rivers, has an opening to the sea, and covers an area of 5,150 square miles (13,210 sq. km). Formed some thirty-six million years ago, it is one of the oldest lakes in the world. This is where Venezuela's first significant oil finds were made, in 1914 and 1922, and the lake is still dotted with oil wells. To the west are the deserts of La Guajira, which straddle the border with Colombia and are the native territory of the Wayúu, Venezuela's largest indigenous group.

The seasonally flooded wetlands of Los Llanos (the plains) cover nearly a quarter of the country, from the Orinoco River Basin west to Colombia. Here there are more cattle than people, and the hardy Llanero cowboys who live in this region make their living by rounding up zebu (also known as humped cattle) on huge, sprawling *hatos* (cattle ranches), and entertain themselves at night with traditional *música llanera* played on the harp, maracas, and *cuatro* (a four-stringed guitar like a ukulele).

Known as the Serengeti of South America, Los Llanos is the best place to see wildlife in Venezuela,

with howler monkeys, armadillos, and capybara—the world's biggest rodents—on land, and rivers full of razor-toothed piranha, anacondas, and spectacled caimans. Bird lovers flock here to see hawks, waders, and around four hundred species of birds.

Beaches and Cities

The Caribbean coast from Maracaibo in the west to Cumaná in the east contains more than 80 percent of the population. The country's largest cities, including Maracay, Valencia, and Caracas, are located along this narrow strip.

Situated in a narrow valley at an altitude of 2,985 ft (910 m), Caracas has a relatively cool year-round climate—considering its tropical location just 10° north of the equator—and is known as "La Ciudad de la Eterna Primavera" ("City of Eternal Spring"). It is separated from the coast by the lushly forested El Ávila mountain, a national park that rises to 9,071 feet (2,765 m) at Pico Naiguata, and has a cable car that takes ten minutes to climb to the iconic but long closed Humboldt Hotel, which overlooks the city.

The country's top beaches can be found along this coast, including the islands off Mochima and the tiny cays of the Morrocoy National Park. Further out are the Robinson Crusoe islands of Los Roques Archipelago, another national park, and the large party island of Margarita, where you can visit a different beach every day.

Tepuis—Islands In Time

In the far south of the country is the Gran Sabana, a region of flat, grassy plains punctuated by huge mesa mountains, or *tepuis*, which are some of the most ancient rock formations in the world. These sandstone mountains are part of the Guiana Shield, and have been eroded down from a vast plateau over the last two to three billion years, leaving unique endemic species on their lofty heights.

The most famous of the *tepuis* is Auyan-*tepui* (Devil Mountain, in the tongue of the native Pémon), from where the world's highest waterfall, Salto Ángel, plummets 3,212 feet (979 m) to the river below.

The highest of the nearly one hundred *tepuis* that dot the Gran Sabana is Mount Roraima, at 9,219 feet (2,810 m). The triple point on the top of the mountain marks the intersection of the Brazilian, Guyanan, and Venezuelan borders, but the only route for hikers to the summit of the mountain is from Venezuela.

CLIMATE

Venezuela's tropical climate is divided into two seasons—rainy and dry—with variations in rainfall dependent on location and altitude. The dry season runs from December to May, and the rainy season from June to November, with lighter rains along the Caribbean coast at Coro and Cumaná, on the deserts of the Paraguana Peninsula, and on the Caribbean islands, and heavier rains in the jungles of the south.

Owing to the country's position on the equator, sunrise takes place at about 6:00 a.m., and sunset at about 6:00 p.m., all year-round. April and August are the hottest months, but even in the rainy season there is significant sunshine between short downpours.

December and January are the coolest months, and at high altitudes in the Andes temperatures drop below freezing all year. In Caracas temperatures can fall quite low at night around Christmas time—a phenomenon named *Pacheco*, after a farmer living on El Ávila mountain who would come down to the city when the nights got too cold. The average daytime temperatures in Mérida are 57–66°F (14–19°C), in Caracas 64–75°F (18–24°C), and on Margarita Island 73–81°F (23–27°C).

The Vargas Floods

On December 15, 1999, one of the worst human tragedies in recent Venezuelan history occurred when fourteen days of heavy rain brought devastating floods and huge mudslides down from El Ávila, wreaking havoc and destruction on the coastal towns and barrios of Vargas State. Houses, hotels, roads, a university complex, and whole families were buried under thousands of tons of mud.

Between 10,000 and 30,000 people died in the Vargas floods. Many thousands more were made homeless and spent months in temporary shelters, with families separated for long periods before they could be rehoused. For some the events of those dark days were so traumatic that they have never returned to their old neighborhoods. Although the government has made huge efforts to rebuild the infrastructure along the coast, and weekenders once again flock to the beaches, the tragedy will never be forgotten, and many hundreds of buildings will never be excavated from the concrete-like mud that now covers them.

THE PEOPLE

Venezuela's twenty-eight million people are a living embodiment of the country's history, reflecting its time as a Spanish colony and the slave economy that sustained it. The Spanish conquistadors who arrived in the 1500s came to conquer and exploit this New World that Christopher Columbus had found, and brought few women with them from Spain. Thus the melting pot of races and cultures began from the time the first Spanish ships touched shore. After the arrival of slaves from Africa—brought to work in mines and on sugar, coffee, and cocoa plantations—another ingredient was added to the mix.

Colonial administrators had to create new terms to document the racial mixing taking place, so *mulatto* was used to describe people of mixed European and African ancestry, *zambo* for mixed African and Amerindian ancestry, and *mestizo* for mixed European and indigenous ancestry (although this term has come to cover all people of mixed-race ancestry). Today some 69 percent of the Venezuelan population are *mestizo* (a mixture of Amerindian, European, and African backgrounds), about 20 percent are white, 9 percent are black, and close to 2 percent are Amerindian.

The main Afro-Venezuelan communities are concentrated along the central coast in towns and villages like Chuao, Puerto Maya, and Chuspa, in the area known as Barlovento, and in towns such as Curiepe and Birongo, where drum dancing and festivals in honor of St. John the Baptist are linked to African beliefs and rituals. There are also important Afro-Venezuelan communities in the area south of Lake Maracaibo, where drum dancing takes place in honor of St. Benedict of Palermo.

After the population was decimated in the long wars of independence, many attempts were made to encourage European immigration, leading to a small group of Black Forest Germans settling in the high valleys of Colonia Tovar in 1843. However, apart from several waves of Canary Islanders and Basques settling in the country, it wasn't until after the Second World War that immigration really picked up, with the arrival of more than 600,000 Spanish, Italians, North Americans, and Portuguese. This was a controlled process, overseen by the government to stimulate agriculture and bring new skills to the country, but it was also a racially motivated program of "*blanquimiento*" (whitening), in the belief that white Europeans would help the progress of the country. Black immigrants were actively excluded. Since then more than a million immigrants have entered the country from Colombia, Ecuador, and Peru, generally to the cities. Skin color is still seen as an indicator of class, with the elite and upper-middle class generally lighter-skinned than the inhabitants of the shantytowns.

Venezuela has a small but significant Amerindian population made up of twenty-eight indigenous tribes, divided between Carib, Arawak, and independent language groups. Largely ignored for many years, Indian rights were formally recognized in the 1999 Constitution. Indigenous groups were given three seats in the National Assembly, and granted rights—in principle—to communally occupied land, although disputes continue over when this will happen and whether all indigenous land claims will be granted.

The largest indigenous group is the Arawak-speaking Wayúu (Guajiros) of Zulia State, who number about 300,000 in Venezuela, with another 150,000 across the border in Colombia. About 80,000

Wayúu live in and around Maracaibo, the capital of Zulia State, and Wayúu women wearing floor-length patterned dresses, known as *mantas*, are a typical sight in the city. The second-largest group is the Warao of the Orinoco River Delta. Some 36,000 Warao continue to live much as they did at the time of the Spanish conquest in *palafito* stilt houses, built over the river, with straw roofs and no walls.

Venezuela—What's In a Name?

There is still some controversy over where the name Venezuela came from. Recent studies have tried to suggest that it was the name of a Carib tribe encountered by the early Spanish adventurers. However, the generally accepted version is that either the Italian banker and seafarer Amerigo Vespucci or the Spanish captain Alonso de Ojeda came up with the name on an expedition to the New World in 1499.

Vespucci wrote in a letter that arriving at the mouth of Lake Maracaibo they were impressed by a "great village" of indigenous houses known as *palafitos* built on stilts over the water. Reminded of the canals of Venice, they named the place Venezuela, or "Little Venice." Finding little in the way of gold or jewels, the explorers obtained some women of "notable beauty and disposition" and continued on their way. The name "Lago de Venezuela" (Lake Venezuela), marking the position of Lake Maracaibo, first appeared on the *Mappa Mundi* made in 1500 by Juan de la Cosa, pilot of the expedition. It later became the name for the whole country.

In the Gran Sabana and the jungles of the south, some 28,000 Pémon practice an ancient culture that is intimately tied up with the high *tepui* mountains that characterize the area. Few Pémon live from hunting and gathering nowadays. Some work as police and park rangers, others in tourism, taking foreigners to the top of *tepuis* that their ancestors believed were the homes of the gods. In the far south Amazonas State, about 18,000 Yanomami and Sanema continue to live a traditional existence in the rain forest, despite encroachments on their remote communities by missionaries and wildcat miners. Other groups also continue to defend their cultural traditions, such as the Yekwana of the Rio Caura, the Panare of Caicara, the Piaroa of the Orinoco and Autana region, and the Kariña of the Mesa de Guanipa.

A BRIEF HISTORY

A rather confused Christopher Columbus arrived in Venezuela on his third voyage, in 1498, after dropping anchor off the coast of the present-day Paria Peninsula. The Admiral of the Ocean Sea had thought that on this voyage he would reach Japan— his goal being to find a sea route to the rich spices of the East—but the quantity of fresh water from the Orinoco River and the wildness of the surroundings as he entered the gulf between Venezuela and Trinidad made him think that he might have found a New World. He wrote in his journal: "I have come to believe that this is a mighty continent which was hitherto unknown. I am greatly supported in this view by reason of this great river, and by this sea which is fresh." However, after setting foot on land on August 7, he changed his mind and called the land "Isla de Gracia" (Island of Grace), describing the natives as "happy, amiable, and hospitable."

A few days later, after detecting the bulge in the earth at the equator in his navigational calculations, he came up with an even stranger concept, suggesting that he was close to the Garden of Eden, whence Adam and Eve had been cast out, because, "If the water does not proceed from the earthly paradise, it seems to be a still greater wonder, for I do not believe that there is any river in the world so large and deep." His answer to all the anomalies on his maps and charts was that the earth was shaped "like a woman's breast" with the Garden of Eden on the nipple. With that odd thought marked down in his log, he sailed west along the coast to Isla Margarita, where he noted the fine pearls and took some samples away with him—a discovery that soon attracted the first Spanish settlers to Venezuela.

Pre-Columbian Venezuela
There is much controversy over the identity of the first inhabitants of Venezuela. For many years it was believed that a gap in the ice sheets 10,000 to 12,000 years ago allowed hunter-gatherers from Siberia to follow large mammals, such as bison, over the Bering

Strait into the Americas, and that from there they went all the way to Tierra del Fuego. But in 1976 an ancient arrowhead found embedded in a mastodon pelvis at Taima Taima, in a desert region near the city of Coro, showed that indigenous people were hunting in that area as early as 13,000 years ago. Although none of the local indigenous groups rose to the heights of the Inca of Peru, or the Mayas and Aztecs of Mexico, there are many lithic and ceramic artifacts in the Andean region that suggest a high level of civilization, including terraced fields and stone structures.

More importantly, the Arawaks and Caribs migrated from the Orinoco region and island-hopped across the Caribbean to Cuba and Puerto Rico, displacing local tribes and imposing their culture. It is from the warlike Caribs that we get the word "cannibal," owing to Spanish reports of Carib warriors feasting on captives.

The Spanish Conquest
The rich pearl beds discovered by Columbus around the small island of Cubagua proved a curse to the indigenous people of the coast, who were raided and enslaved by the Spaniards who came after him in the 1500s. Taken in chains to Cubagua, just off the coast of Isla Margarita, they were forced to dive for pearls and build the city of Nueva Cádiz; founded in 1515, it was known as the first Spanish city in South America, and quickly became one of the richest.

By 1539 the pearl beds were no longer producing, the city was abandoned, and the rush to open up the mainland had begun with the founding of Cumaná in 1521—despite heavy resistance by local tribes—

and the city of Coro, in 1527, which became the capital of the province of Venezuela.

In 1528, the Holy Roman Emperor Charles V leased the new province to a German banking family of the name of Welser. Instead of exploring and settling the country, however, the German-backed governors, Ambrosius Ehinger, Nikolaus Federmann, and Philipp von Hutten, spent their time searching in vain for the mythic city of gold, El Dorado, and decimating the indigenous tribes they encountered.

The Welser family also brought missionaries to spread the Catholic faith among the Indians of the interior, and the first African slaves to toil away in the copper mines and on cacao and sugar plantations, thus establishing the colonial system that was to persist until independence.

The Move to Independence

The first moves toward independence began with an unsuccessful slave revolt in Coro in 1795 by José Leonardo Chirino that was inspired by the revolution in Haiti (1791–1804) against France. That was followed in 1806 by an ill-fated invasion of the country by Francisco de Miranda with five hundred volunteers he had recruited in the USA.

Miranda was an extraordinary individual who had fought in the French Revolution, faced the guillotine under the Terror, and fled to Russia, where he had become the lover of Catherine the Great. A brave soldier, statesman, and free thinker, Miranda was a Byronic hero inspired with a passion to free his homeland, which he saw as groaning under the weight of onerous taxes and limitations on trade imposed from Madrid and where *criollos* (Spaniards born in South America) were barred from the top jobs, to which only *peninsulares* (those born in Spain) had access.

Miranda spent many years in London planning his return and trying to get the British government involved in a military venture, but the landing in 1806 was a complete failure because the local population were not prepared to join his uprising. In the end, sixty-three of the US volunteers were captured and the officers hanged, although Miranda himself was able to escape.

The First Republic

The key event that laid the groundwork for independence was Napoleon Bonaparte's invasion of Spain in 1808. Deposing the Spanish King Charles IV and his heir Ferdinand VII, Bonaparte placed his brother Joseph on the Spanish throne.

Venezuela, like many of the Spanish colonies, declared its independence of this usurper and in 1810 a young aristocrat called Simón Bolívar traveled to London to ask Miranda to lead the First Republic.

Back in Venezuela, Miranda had some military successes against the Spanish Royalists but after a serious setback he sued for peace, which Simón Bolívar and other young leaders saw as a betrayal. As Miranda waited to board a British ship to take him back to London he was seized and handed over to the Spanish, who sent him to Cádiz, where he died in La Carraca prison in 1816 at the age of sixty-six, his remains thrown unceremoniously into a mass grave. Today, Miranda is hailed as El Precursor (The Forerunner) and an empty tomb awaits him in the National Pantheon in Caracas.

SIMÓN BOLÍVAR

Simón José Antonio de la Santísima Trinidad Bolívar y Palacios Ponte y Blanco was born into one of the richest families in the country. He went on to lead the wars of independence against Spain that liberated not only Venezuela but also present-day Colombia, Panama, Ecuador, Bolivia, and Peru.

Despite his great achievements on the battle-field, Bolívar was unable to hold together his vision for a unified Gran Colombia of South American states and died in 1830 a broken and disillusioned man, stating, just before he died, "He who serves a revolution plows the sea." In 1999 the country was renamed the República Bolivariana de Venezuela by President Chávez, whose political philosophy he calls "Bolivarianism" in honor of the great man.

This is nothing new. Venezuelan presidents have been lauding the achievements of Bolívar for more than a hundred years, and many have used his name to give weight to their political projects. He is known as *El Libertador* (the Liberator) and *El Padre de la Patria* (Father of the Nation). His remains are in a grand tomb in the Panteón Nacional in Caracas, alongside the tombs of other independence heroes, including his Irish aide-de-camp and biographer Daniel Florence O'Leary. Almost every city, town, and village in Venezuela has a central plaza with a statue of Bolívar, standing or on horseback, and the national currency, the Bolívar Fuerte, is named after him.

Bolívar Takes Command

After taking control of the independence forces, Simón Bolívar declared a "war to the death" against the Spanish Royalists, and in 1818 formed a new government in Angostura (now Ciudad Bolívar).

Joining up with the hardy horsemen of Los Llanos led by General José Antonio Páez, and bringing on board British and Irish fighters in the British Legion,

Bolívar then marched his army over the Andes into Colombia in 1819—a surprise move that allowed him to take the whole province. Returning victorious to Venezuela, he led the decisive battle of Carabobo on June 24, 1821, which destroyed the main Spanish army.

Bolívar then led successful campaigns in Peru in 1824 to drive out the Spanish for good and form the Republic of Gran Colombia—covering present-day Venezuela, Colombia, Panama, Ecuador, Peru, and Bolivia, which is named after him.

The Death of a Dream

In December 1830 Simón Bolívar died of tuberculosis in Santa Marta. He was on his way to London, unwanted in the lands he had liberated from Spain, his health wrecked by countless marches, defeats, and victories, his vast wealth spent, his dream of a unified bloc of South American states in tatters. In the same year José Antonio Páez, Centaur of the Llanos and hero of the independence wars, declared Venezuela a sovereign state and became its first president.

NATIONAL SYMBOLS

The Venezuelan flag was originally designed by the romantic and revolutionary Francisco de Miranda in 1806, during his first failed attempt at liberating the country from Spanish control. It consists of three equal horizontal bands. The yellow band at the top represents the gold or the wealth of the country, the blue band is the sea separating the Americas from Spain, and the red at the bottom is the blood that was spilled to gain independence.

The flag originally had seven white stars in an arc across the central band, representing the seven provinces at independence. In 2006, the government added an eighth star to represent the province of Guayana. The national seal, or coat of arms, that appears in the top left-hand corner contains the dates of the Declaration of Independence on April 19, 1810, and the start of the Federation War on February 20, 1859.

A sheaf of wheat represents the abundance of the earth and the union of the states, and two flags with swords symbolize the triumph of the Independence struggle. The galloping white horse on a blue background represents freedom and the march of progress. It was shown facing right and looking back to the left but in 2006 a change was made to show the horse galloping and facing left. This is the usual position for animals in heraldry, but the change was considered by some critics of the government as a political decision to symbolize the left-wing ideology of the Chavez government.

Rise of the Caudillos

The next seventy years were marked by continuing wars and upheavals as a series of *caudillos* (strongmen) battled for control of the state. The Federal Wars from 1859 to 1863 between liberals and conservatives again decimated the small population of Venezuela, which at that time numbered no more than a million people.

A brief period of calm and progress came under the progressive rule of the Liberal leader Antonio Guzmán Blanco from 1870 to 1877 and again from 1879 to 1884. The "Illustrious American," as he liked

to be called, introduced compulsory free schooling and tried to transform the capital city into a mini-Paris with French-style theaters, salons, and the Capitol building as the seat of government. Many bronze statues of Simón Bolívar were erected under Guzmán Blanco, and the National Pantheon was built to house the remains of the main independence fighters.

The Tyrant of the Andes

Initially leading the army of another *caudillo,* Cipriano Castro, Juan Vicente Gómez was an illiterate cattle herder from Táchira. He took Caracas by force in 1899 for Castro, and in 1908 seized power for himself, ruling the country for the next twenty-seven years as if it were his own private cattle ranch. Cunning and cruel, he was an unrepentant lothario: he had fifteen children by his two mistresses and as many as eighty other illegitimate offspring.

Congress showered him with medals and dubbed him El Benemérito (the Meritorious One), while his opponents called him El Bagre (the Catfish), for his signature moustache and cold eyes. No opposition to his rule was allowed, and student activists had to operate clandestinely or spend time in prison. His vast wealth was initially focused on property, but the discovery of oil in Maracaibo in 1914 soon transformed the economy of Venezuela and by the time Gómez died in 1936 Venezuela was the number one oil exporter in the world—a position it would hold until the emergence of Saudi Arabia as a world petro-power.

A Brief Flowering of Democracy, and Dictatorship

The country's first fully democratic elections— organized in 1947 by Rómulo Betancourt of the left-of-center Acción Democrática party—were won by the novelist Rómulo Gallegos. After attempts at reform he was toppled by a military junta led by the diminutive General Marcos Pérez Jiménez.

Pérez controlled the country for ten years. In that time he oversaw an ambitious program of public works, including great highways linking the main cities, public housing projects, and the cable-car systems on the mountain of El Ávila and in Mérida.

Eventually, his feared secret police were not enough to suppress public protests calling for democracy to be restored, and on January 23, 1958, he fled to the USA. There he remained until 1963, when he was extradited back and found guilty of embezzling 200 million US dollars.

Democracy and the Punto Fijo Pact

When Rómulo Betancourt won the elections in 1959 the two main parties, Acción Democratica (AD) and the Social Christian Party (COPEI) agreed to alternate power under a deal known as the Punto Fijo Pact, which was to last thirty years.

Under Betancourt, Venezuela founded the Organization of Petroleum Exporting Countries with Iran, Iraq, Kuwait, and Saudi Arabia in 1960. This led to increased oil wealth in the country, especially in the boom years under President Carlos Andrés Pérez (1974–79), who nationalized the oil industry, created PDVSA, the state oil company, and ushered in a period known as "Venezuela Saudita," when newly rich Venezuelans flew to Miami to do their weekend shopping and became known as *damedos* ("give me two").

The oil-profits party came to an end under President Luís Herrera Campins in 1983, when there was a massive devaluation of the currency and savings were wiped out. The event is still known as Black Friday, and it ushered in a massive economic hangover that continued into the second presidency of Carlos Andrés Pérez (1989–93).

The Caracazo

The decision by Carlos Andrés Pérez to instigate an IMF-imposed austerity package, the end of subsidies on food, and a hike in gas prices at the pumps led to widespread unrest, and on February

27, 1989, the situation exploded into rioting and looting in the capital. These disturbances became known as "El Caracazo." Dramatic scenes of looters carrying whole sides of beef back up to the *barrios* were shown on national TV, and the president declared martial law. Thousands of people died over the next few days in the military crackdown, most of them from the poorest *barrios* of the city.

The End of Punto Fijo and the Rise of Chávez
It was the Caracazo that spurred on a young military officer, Hugo Rafael Chávez Frías, to lead a military coup on February 4, 1992. President Pérez narrowly escaped capture by the rebel soldiers, fleeing from the Miraflores presidential palace just as a tank tried to break down the doors. Chávez, seeing that continuing the fighting would only lead to more bloodshed, surrendered, but in a history-defining moment he asked to be allowed to speak to the TV reporters and tell his fellow rebels, who were still fighting, to lay down their arms. In his short speech he acknowledged defeat but finished with the words *por ahora* (for now), suggesting that all was not over. Chávez was immediately imprisoned but became an overnight sensation, a rallying point for all those sick of government corruption, particularly after President Pérez was impeached for embezzling state funds.

The first person to break the Punto Fijo Pact was not an outsider but the elderly President Caldera, a founder of COPEI, who had served as president between 1969 and 1974 but who ran in the 1994 election as an independent. It was Caldera who pardoned Chávez and handed over the presidential sash when the ex-soldier won a landslide victory to become president in 1999.

Birth of the Bolivarian Republic

The wave of elation that greeted Chávez's election victory gave the new president sufficient momentum to set up a Constituent Assembly to rewrite the constitution. He also changed the country's name to the Bolivarian Republic of Venezuela, in honor of his idol Simón Bolívar. It became clear that things were going to change and that the changes would be on a scale unseen before.

Consequently, Chávez won an even bigger majority in the 2000 presidential election and it

seemed that the corruption and cronyism of the Punto Fijo Pact years was being replaced by a fairer system, where the oil wealth would be shared more equally and poverty reduced. Not bad for a poor boy who had grown up in a mud hut in the dusty town of Sabaneta in Barinas State.

However, Chávez's support of Cuba's Fidel Castro, his antagonism toward the USA, and what he saw as its "meddling in Latin America," added to his fiery rhetoric against "savage neoliberalism," quickly won him enemies among the business elite and in private media outlets. There was a polarization in the country between those who supported Chávez unquestioningly—generally the poorest in society who had the most to gain—and those who would never warm to his homegrown brand of Bolivarian socialism—generally from the middle and upper classes who had the most to lose.

Tackling Poverty, Making Enemies

When Chávez came to power some 80 percent of Venezuelans lived in poverty, while a moneyed elite lived in luxury apartment complexes and played golf at the exclusive country club. He chose to bypass the crumbling public health and education systems in place and set up schemes that he called *misiones* (missions), aimed at tackling the problems of illiteracy, malnutrition, and poor health at the source, in the sprawling shantytowns.

Misión Robinson, named after Simón Bolívar's teacher, provided basic literacy and numerical skills and was able to raise Venezuela's literacy levels to 93 percent, while Misión Ribas offered a second chance at a high school education for those who had missed out.

To tackle malnutrition a system of subsidized food outlets and weekly markets was set up, known as Misión Mercal, which later provided a way to pressurize private food companies to bring down prices, but has not stopped shortages of some basic foodstuffs.

These moves were combined with an expropriation and redistribution program of "idle lands," the renationalization of state companies that had been privatized under previous administrations, and the expropriation of private firms in key areas. Not surprisingly, the large family firms affected by these changes saw themselves under attack, and a backlash against the Chávez regime began.

Private newspapers and TV channels also began to criticize the government, leading to a media war with Chávez, who responded by pulling government advertisements from private media outlets, pumping money into state channels and newspapers, and starting his own Sunday TV and radio show called *Aló, Presidente* (Hello, President).

Polarization

In the meantime, the president declared himself a twenty-first-century socialist, strengthened his alliance with Cuba, reached out to Iran, Russia, and China, and stepped up his attacks on the USA, and George W. Bush in particular. The result was a polarization of the country and several attempts to unseat him.

The most serious attempt took place on April 11, 2002, when nineteen people from both sides of the political divide were killed during an opposition march. Some top generals called for the president to resign, and he was whisked away to a tiny Caribbean island. The next day an interim government was sworn in, led by businessman Pedro Carmona, whose first act was to cancel constitutional guarantees and suspend the Supreme Court. But nobody had planned for the response of Chávez's supporters, thousands of whom surrounded the presidential palace and demanded to see Chávez. It all ended when a group of soldiers took control of the palace and Chávez returned in triumph just forty-eight hours after he was ousted.

Since then there has been an unsuccessful oil strike to try to bring down the government, a referendum to try to have the president removed, which also failed, the 2006 presidential election that he won with 63 percent of the vote, and a 2009 referendum on allowing the president to run for office indefinitely, which Chávez also won.

As this book goes to press, President Chávez is battling cancer. This has put the president's ability to fight the October 2012 election in doubt, even though polls put him ahead of the unified opposition candidate Henrique Capriles Radonski, aged thirty-nine, who is the best-placed candidate to defeat Chávez in thirteen years. With no other candidate in his socialist PSUV party having the same charisma as Chávez it seems likely he will contest the election himself, whatever his medical condition.

GOVERNMENT

Venezuela is a Democratic Federal Republic with a president elected by universal suffrage every six years. The president is both chief of state and head of government, and has the power to appoint the vice president and a cabinet of ministers.

A referendum in 2009 removed the limits on how many times a president can run for election, allowing President Chávez to run for a third term in October 2012.

The legislative branch consists of a unicameral Asamblea Nacional (National Assembly) made up of 167 deputies who are elected every five years, including three seats reserved for representatives of Venezuela's indigenous peoples.

In 2005 the opposition boycotted parliamentary elections, but in 2010 they participated under the umbrella organization Mesa de la Unidad Democrática (MUD) (Coalition for Democratic Unity), gaining sixty-four seats and nearly 50 percent of the total vote.

THE ECONOMY

Venezuela is the oil giant of South America and a founding member of the Organization of Petroleum Exporting Countries (OPEC). Ever since the big US oil firms set up shop in the country under the dictator Juan Vicente Gomez, the biggest business in Venezuela has been the oil business, making up over 90 percent of exports and 50 percent of government income.

The huge revenues generated from being the sixth-largest oil exporter in the world and the focus on large state-run heavy industries, such as steel and aluminum, have come at the expense of investment in other areas of the economy, such as agriculture and manufacturing. This has resulted in a situation where Venezuela relies heavily on imported food and goods.

The traditional dominance of US brands and investment by US multinationals in the country has been challenged by the government of President Hugo Chávez over the last thirteen years as he has sought to reduce the country's reliance on the USA as a trading partner.

There has also been a policy of renationalization of key industries, including telephone, electricity, cement and steel firms, the renegotiation of oil, gas, and mining deals with multinationals on more advantageous terms, and the expropriation of private companies considered strategically important.

In a bid to increase Venezuela's non-US trading ties, there has been a greater emphasis on trade with the South American trading bloc Mercosur, principally with Brazil and Argentina, and with political allies in Cuba, Nicaragua, Ecuador, and Bolivia.

The most important change under President Chávez has been the increasing number of ambitious joint ventures with Russia, China, and Iran, particularly in the oil and gas sectors.

chapter two

VALUES &
ATTITUDES

THE FAMILY

The family is at the heart of Venezuelan life, and in an uncertain world, where things can get tough, it is the main support system. The definition of "family" here goes beyond the nuclear family concept of parents and children. It includes grandparents, aunts, uncles, cousins, and even close family friends who might have a hand in helping to care for children.

Large extended families, especially poorer ones, often live together under one roof. Most young adults continue to live with their parents after their education is finished, and sometimes even after marriage, again for financial reasons. It is also typical for grandparents or elderly relatives to remain in the family house or be cared for by younger relatives rather than go to an old people's home; this goes for rich families as well as poor.

Even living apart, people spend a great deal of time with the members of their extended family, often dropping in unannounced for coffee and a chat. There is a constant round of parties and celebrations to cement family bonds, such as birthdays, marriages, christenings, *quinceañeras* (the important fifteenth birthday parties for girls), and Christmas festivities.

Respect for the family and for elders is instilled at a young age. You will hear young children asking a parent, uncle, aunt, or godparent for a blessing and receiving one in return: "*Bendición, Tío*" (Blessing, Uncle), "*Dios te bendiga, Hijo*" (God bless you, Child). Venezuelans are also very physically affectionate within the family.

MEN, WOMEN, AND *MACHISMO*

There is a sense that men are men and women are women in Venezuela, where the traditional concepts of gallantry and *machismo* have survived into the twenty-first century. An oft-quoted Venezuelan expression to describe gender roles in romance is: "*El hombre propone y la mujer dispone*" (The man suggests and the woman decides). This is reflected in courtship, where men are expected to make the first move, on dates, where men are expected to pay for everything, and at dances, where men lead.

In many households, this division is seen in the fact that boys are spoiled by their mothers and female relatives, who don't expect them to cook or clean, while girls are expected to learn all the skills of running a home.

Things are changing, however. The traditional roles of men as sole providers of family income and women as stay-at-home housekeepers, cooks, and child caregivers are no longer sustainable in an economic situation where both partners have to work to make ends meet. Women have adapted rapidly to meet the changing demands of modern society, and this can be seen at the universities, where women make up 52 percent of the students, and at work, where they hold jobs on a par with men in nearly every profession apart from politics.

Men, meanwhile, continue to expect a traditional arrangement in the home, and have been slower to adapt. The practical result of this is that many women have to shoulder the burden of holding down a full-time job while still doing the majority of the cooking and cleaning and looking after the children.

The number of absentee fathers and the high murder rate among young men in the *barrios* means that many poorer households have to survive without a male provider.

Another element of machismo to survive into the twenty-first century is the slightly comic approach to the opposite sex by some men on the street, especially when in groups, who will compliment any and every good-looking or curvaceous woman who walks by.

It's a cliché, but nearly everyone in Venezuela knows a man who has had children with multiple partners. The general view seems to be that it's not the children's fault if their dad is a rogue, and when a father doesn't live up to expectations it is not uncommon for children to be brought up by aunts, grandparents, godmothers, or family friends.

SOCIAL CLASS AND STATUS
However hard the government has been working over the last thirteen years to eliminate extreme poverty, the huge gulf that still exists between the very rich and the very poor in Venezuela is apparent

from a quick scan of the Caracas skyline, where
luxury apartment complexes set around swimming
pools are interspersed with hillsides covered in
shanties. Areas like the Country Club in the center
of the city, with its gated mansions and exclusive golf
club, are a world away from the concrete floors and
zinc roofs of populous *barrios* such as Petare and
Guarataro. Social class in the big cities is represented
very physically by where you can afford to live as
much as by what you have, and one of the first
questions asked of new acquaintances is what part
of town they come from.

Loveable Rogues

An English friend of mine once spent Christmas Eve
with a Venezuelan girlfriend at her grandmother's
place, and was surprised to learn that a man who
was dancing the night away with all the ladies had
fathered six children with four women. Even more
surprising was that all the women and children were
present, and getting along famously. His eldest child
was twenty-six, the youngest six months. His new
girlfriend was younger than his eldest child.

A Venezuelan I knew was with her family at the
bedside of her ninety-year-old grandfather, who
was dying in a hospital. The old man called into the
room a young woman with two small children, and
asked the family to recognize the children as his,
and to look after them. After the shock had worn
off—and with some bemusement among the male
relatives at how he had managed such a feat at his
age—arrangements were made for the children to
be cared for.

Other important status symbols are cars—particularly the extravagant models such as Hummers and other excessive four-by-four monsters. The number of new models on the city streets is a clear reminder of the level of wealth being generated by the oil industry, while the number of old cars that should have been scrapped years ago is a reminder of how cheap the subsidized oil is.

The fashion for showing off one's wealth goes back to the 1970s, when for ten years the oil boom made Venezuelans the richest people per capita in South America, and the country got a reputation for excess and ostentation. As we have seen, the Venezuelans flying to Miami on weekend shopping trips were known as *damedos,* because of the phrase, "*Esta barato, dame dos*" ("That's cheap, give me two").

In recent years the Venezuelan moneyed elite have been joined by the members of a new class, described in the media as the *Boliburguesia (*Bolivarian bourgeoisie), or *Boligarquia* (Bolivarian oligarchs), who have benefited financially from the political and economic changes in the country. Rich kids who flaunt their status are known as *sifrinos* (snobs), while insults leveled at the poor are to call them *marginales* (marginals), a reference to the *barrios* as marginal communities, or *monos* (monkeys), a slur considered racist by most Venezuelans.

ATTITUDES TOWARD RACE
Venezuela is a *mestizo* (mixed-race) nation, born of the intermingling of Spanish settlers, the indigenous first inhabitants of the continent, and slaves brought from Africa. The result is every shade and hue of skin

color from white to black, with the vast majority of the population an attractive shade of *cafe con leche* (coffee with milk).

In general, upper- and middle-class Venezuelans are lighter-skinned—a legacy of the Spanish conquest and later immigration by Europeans and North Americans—while the darkest skin tones are found along the central coast, to the south of Lake Maracaibo and other areas where African slaves were brought to work on the coffee, cocoa, and sugar plantations.

Ask most Venezuelans if there is racism in their country and they will say no, pointing to the fact that black, brown, white, and indigenous Venezuelans live together, work together, intermarry without problem, and are equal under the law. They will also point out that if a small amount of racism does exist it never comes close to the rhetoric of race hatred spouted by some groups in the USA or northern Europe.

This attitude of racial harmony was summed up by Simón Bolívar, who famously said, "We were all born of one mother America, though our fathers had different origins, and we all have differently colored skins." Another popular quote is "*Somos todos criollos*" (We are all Creoles), meaning that we were all born here, and we are all equal.

However, skin color is linked to perceptions of social class, and there are examples of darker-skinned Venezuelans being refused entry to exclusive clubs and bars on the flimsiest of excuses. In the past it was rare to see dark skins in the media, with white-skinned, blue-eyed blondes on the covers of glossy magazines or hosting TV shows, but since President

Chávez came to power there has been a shift toward a range of models and hosts who better reflect the reality of the general population.

THE BODY BEAUTIFUL

The cult of beauty is almost a religion in Venezuela, and beauty pageants are a national obsession. People invest a lot of time and effort on their personal appearance, and women will spend hours at the hairdresser each week, having manicures, pedicures, and other treatments to enhance their god-given attributes and look as feminine as possible. Clothes are worn tight to show off curves—either natural or surgically enhanced—and short hems and long hair are the norm.

Plastic surgery is a normal part of growing up for girls who can afford it—and many who can't. There is no embarrassment over it, and girls wear the bandages on their noses with pride after rhinoplasty. Banks even advertise loans specifically for breast implants.

Venezuelans are some of the largest per capita consumers of cosmetics, and a survey in 2000 found Venezuelans to be the vainest people in the world, with 65 percent of women who took part saying they thought about their looks all the time (only 27 percent of US women felt the same).

The desire to look good is reflected in high gym membership, the joggers doing early morning circuits of the parks, and the weekend hikers walking up and down the steep trail from Altamira to Sabas Nieves on the mountain of Ávila.

The Record-Breaking Beauty Business

It is a huge source of national pride that Venezuela has won six Miss Universe titles, six Miss Worlds, six Miss Internationals, and a Miss Earth, placing it in the record books for the country with the most beauty queens.

In 2009, eighteen-year-old Stefania Fernandez made Miss Universe history when she was crowned by fellow Venezuelan Dayana Mendoza, the 2008 winner. It was the first time any country had had back-to-back victories in the contest.

The obsession with beauty queens extends to the country's oil tankers, which are named after past winners, but the strangest accolade must go to the "*Reina Pepiada*" (the Curvy Queen), a popular *arepa* (see pages 99 and 105) filling of shredded chicken, mashed avocado, mayonnaise, and peas, which was named in honor of Susana Dujim, Miss World 1955.

Since 1981, the man behind the Miss Venezuela organization has been Cuban émigré Osmel Sousa, who runs the Miss Venezuela School like a military boot camp, but with high heels. Under Sousa's critical gaze, potential winners learn how to walk, talk, and act like a Miss, and if necessary go under the knife. One of the few girls to refuse surgery was Ivian Sarcos, who won Venezuela's sixth Miss World title in 2011.

Brains and Beauty Overcome Adversity

Hollywood couldn't come up with a more dramatic fairy tale than the story of Ivian Sarcos and the incredible drive, determination, and luck that saw her crowned Miss World on November 6, 2011, in front of a global TV audience of a billion people.

Combining a rare beauty with a fine brain, Ivian Sarcos is a human resources graduate who grew up a world away from the glitter and sparkle of the beauty industry. Born the youngest of thirteen children in the Llanos town of Guanare, she was orphaned at the age of eight. Taken in by nuns, she considered becoming a nun herself before deciding to follow a university career. She paid for her education by waiting tables in a fast-food restaurant and later working in a store in Caracas. It was there in 2009 that she was spotted by a friend of Osmel Sousa, the head of the Miss Venezuela organization.

Her story illustrates the incredible obstacles that many young Venezuelan women have to overcome and the drive that pushes them to improve their lives through hard work and study.

RELIGION

Venezuela has been a Catholic country since the arrival of the Spanish conquistadors, and more than

90 percent of Venezuelans identify themselves as Roman Catholic. For many Venezuelans, Catholicism is something they are born with rather than a devout calling. Church services don't overflow on Sundays; people practice family planning, have children out of wedlock, and happily eat meat on Fridays. But belief in the power of religion is strong. Even Venezuelans who don't go to church will carry images of saints and virgins for "protection," or place a candle in front of a Catholic saint to say a prayer and ask a favor.

Catholic fiestas and the procession of saints, especially locally revered saints like the Chiquinquira Virgin in Maracaibo and the Virgin of the Valley in Margarita, attract huge crowds, and the visits by Pope John Paul II in 1985 and 1996 saw hundreds of thousands come out to see him pass by.

Baptists, Jehovah's Witnesses, and Pentecostal groups minister to about 8 percent of the population, and are a growing presence. One evangelical group that has been growing fast, particularly in poor areas, is the Brazilian-based Pentecostal Church Pare de Sufrir, which uses TV ads to attract new worshipers and preaches that financial prosperity can be achieved through prayer.

There are small but significant Jewish communities in Caracas and other cities, and Muslims, mainly of Lebanese origin, are found in Caracas, Margarita, and Punto Fijo.

Some indigenous groups have converted to Christianity, but many, such as the Wayuu in Zulia State, the Pémon in the Gran Sabana, and the

Yanomami in the Orinoco region conserve traditional beliefs and shamanistic rituals. The homegrown María Lionza cult, a syncretic religion sometimes described as Venezuelan voodoo, has followers all over the country but is focused on the mountain of Sorte, near Chivacoa, where rituals involving spirit possession take place in front of images of mythical and historical figures.

NATIONAL PRIDE

Venezuelans are intensely proud of their country and its national heroes, starting with the ultimate icon, Simón Bolívar, who appears on the highest-denomination bill, the 100 BsF. Bolívar's teacher Simón Rodríguez (1769–1854) is on the 50 BsF; the independence heroine Luisa Cáceres de Arismendi

(1799–1866), who was imprisoned in a fortress on Margarita Island, on the 20 BsF; Guaicaipuro (died 1568), the chief of the Teques Indians who fought the Spanish conquistadors in Caracas, on the 10 BsF; the black independence hero Pedro Camejo (1790–1821), also known as "Negro Primero," who was killed at the Battle of Carabobo, on the 5 BsF; and the lover of Catherine the Great of Russia and independence hero Francisco de Miranda (1750– 1816) on the 2 BsF. Another national hero is the politician and author Rómulo Gallegos (1884–1969).

All these historical figures are a source of intense national pride, but Venezuelans are also proud of contemporary talents, such as the fashion designer Carolina Herrera, the supermodel and Hollywood actress Patricia Velásquez, and the actor Edgar Ramirez, who has played opposite Keira Knightley, Matt Damon, and Liam Neeson.

The conductor Gustavo Dudamel, and José Antonio Abreu, who founded a system of youth orchestras for thousands of Venezuela's most disadvantaged children, are also highly esteemed.

The famed beauty of Venezuelan women and the country's success in international beauty pageants are a tremendous source of pride, as are its geographical beauties, such as Salto Ángel, the highest waterfall in the world, and the Caribbean beaches of Margarita and Los Roques.

ATTITUDES TOWARD THE LAW

With a history of corruption at all levels of government and an endemic fear of authority figures, especially the police and the National Guard, Venezuelans see the law as something that does not always work as it should on paper and therefore hold the view that bending the rules is justified in some situations.

This relaxed attitude to rules and regulations is immediately apparent on the roads, where drivers will justify running red lights, especially at night, because of security concerns over carjackings. However, drunk driving, speaking on a cell phone in traffic, and throwing garbage out of the car window are common, even though everybody knows they are illegal.

There is an idea that you need to be *vivo* (sharp) and *listo* (clever) to get by, even if it means cutting corners, and only a *gafo* (idiot) would blindly follow the rules while everybody else is breaking them.

ATTITUDES TOWARD FOREIGNERS

Venezuelans have a long history of welcoming foreigners to their shores, including the thousands of Italians and Spanish who came in search of a new life after the Second World War, and the US oil workers who came in droves in the 1950s and '60s.

Hey, Gringo!

Venezuelans can be quite familiar when addressing foreigners, and on the street a number of terms are used to get your attention. Anybody foreign looking might be called *gringo* or *gringa*, even if they don't come from the USA. Less common is *musiu* (mister), a Venezuelan pronunciation of *monsieur* that I was sometimes called if I pointed out I was European. Blonde or blue-eyed visitors may be called *catire* or *catira*.

No offense is intended by the use of these terms—unless the delivery is aggressive—it's just that Venezuelans have a habit of giving everybody a nickname, a consequence of big families in the past with so many kids called María and José. Anybody carrying a few extra pounds might be called "*gordo/a*" ("fatty") and those looking slim "*flaco/a*" ("skinny").

Diminutives are often used to make the terms more appealing, but it can still be unsettling the first time you walk into a store and the assistant says: "*Epale, gordito. En que te puedo ayudar?*" (Hey, chunky. How can I help you?)

Many of those migrants married into Venezuelan families and stayed here, and their contribution was warmly welcomed. The Italians brought with them the Gaggia coffee machines that you find in every bakery; the Spanish opened seafood restaurants and tasca bars, serving beer and traditional Spanish savory snacks; the Portuguese set up corner stores called *abastos*; and US oil workers contributed to the language with a legacy of Spanglish words that are still used today.

The same hospitality greets modern visitors, who will find Venezuelans to be disarmingly direct and spontaneous, as willing to share a cold beer with a stranger as a member of the family.

The political discourse may have heated up in recent years between President Chávez and his US counterparts, but that has had very little effect on relations between ordinary Venezuelans and foreign visitors.

That's not to say that Venezuelans are not sensitive to criticism, because they are. How you are treated in Venezuela depends very much on how you treat the people you meet. If you are prepared to join in with the group, try out some Spanish, and have a stab at dancing salsa rather than just insisting you can't, you will get a much warmer welcome.

WORK ETHIC AND TIMEKEEPING

Life is precarious for many people, and at all levels of society Venezuelans are striving to improve their situation through hard work and education. Unemployment is high, and many people have to make ends meet in the informal economy, juggling two or more small jobs rather than a single well-paid one. It is typical for Venezuelans to have two jobs and study at the same time, putting themselves through night school to improve their job prospects.

Traffic problems can make commuting a nightmare, and many workers from the suburbs have to start their day extremely early to be at work on time. The traffic problems that plague the cities, especially Caracas, have led to a situation where timekeeping and punctuality have become fairly flexible concepts. Venezuelans rarely arrive exactly on time. It is in any case considered rude to turn up for a dinner invitation on the dot, because the hosts will still be getting ready.

If somebody does expect to start an event at an exact time they might specify *hora británica* (British time).

The attitude to timekeeping can be frustrating for northern Europeans, and can lead to misunderstandings.

chapter three

CUSTOMS & TRADITIONS

Venezuela still has a living calendar of customs and traditions that have a real meaning for the people who participate in them, and give shape to their year. For the Devil Dancers who don masks and attack the Church during the Feast of Corpus Christi there is a spiritual danger to their acts, and they wear amulets and receive blessings from the priest to keep them safe. Equally, for the drummers of Barlovento or Chuao who play for St. John the Baptist on his day, the music and dancing are a direct connection with their roots in Africa.

FESTIVALS AND HOLIDAYS

Días feriados (public holidays) and *fiestas* (feast days or festivals) are taken very seriously in Venezuela. Sometimes, especially from the start of the year through to Semana Santa (Holy Week/Easter) in March or April, it can seem as if the country is on one long holiday—after Christmas and New Year, things don't get back to normal in many businesses until January 15, and before you know it Carnival has arrived.

It is also typical for businesses to shut down early before public holidays, as many people travel long distances to visit relatives, or take the family to the beach or the mountains for a barbecue and a swim.

Not surprisingly, traffic is generally gridlocked before and after Christmas, Carnival, and Holy Week, and bus terminals and airports get quite frantic as the crowds compete for limited seats.

When a public holiday falls on a Thursday or a Tuesday, many people will take an extra day off, known as a *puente* (bridge), so they can have a four-day weekend.

PUBLIC HOLIDAYS

January 1	New Year's Day
Carnival	Monday and Tuesday before Lent
Semana Santa	Maundy (Holy) Thursday, Good Friday
April 19	Proclamation of Independence (1810)
May 1	Labor Day
June 24	Battle of Carabobo. The decisive battle in Venezuela's war of independence against Spanish control, celebrated with military parades
July 5	Independence Day. Signing of Declaration of Independence in 1811
July 24	Simón Bolívar's Birthday
October 12	Day of Indigenous Resistance (formerly Columbus Day)
December 25	Christmas Day

OTHER HOLIDAYS AND FESTIVALS

January 6	Los Reyes Magos (Three Kings, Epiphany)
January 14	Feria de la Divina Pastora (Divine Shepherdess), Barquisimeto
January 20	Feria de San Sebastian, San Cristóbal. Two weeks of music, sports, and bullfights

March 19	San José (St. Joseph's Day). Bullfights in Maracay
May 3	Cruz de Mayo
May 15	San Isidro Labrador. Mérida State
May, June	Corpus Christi. Movable feast, ninth Thursday after Holy Thursday
June 13	San Antonio. Tamunangue dancing in El Tocuyo, Quíbor, Sanare
June 23-24	Fiesta de San Juan Bautista (St. John the Baptist)
August 8	Nuestra Señora de las Nieves (Our Lady of the Snows), Ciudad Bolívar
September 8	La Virgen del Valle (Virgin of the Valley). Patroness of Margarita honored with processions at her shrine in El Valle and in Puerto La Cruz
September 8–11	La Virgen de Coromoto, Guanare. Chief Coromoto's conversion in 1651 and Coronation of the Virgin celebrated
October 12	Cult of María Lionza in Sorte, Yaracuy State
November 18	Feria de la Chinita. Maracaibo celebrates its patron, the Virgin of Chiquinquirá (La Chinita), with ten days of festivities, music, and parades
December 24	*Misa de Gallo* (Midnight Mass)
December 27–29	San Benito. The black saint is honored in Zulia and Mérida
December 28	Día de Los Inocentes (Innocents' Day)— expect practical jokes on the Venezuelan version of April Fools' Day

Navidad (Christmas. December 24-25)
In December Venezuelan children are busy writing
letters to El Niño Jesús (Baby Jesus), listing the
presents they are hoping to receive. Otherwise the
days before Christmas are a time for dancing to

gaitas music from Zulia, reunions with friends, and parties at work. In many offices, workers set up a "Secret Santa"—you take the name of one colleague out of a hat and buy them a present to leave on their desk or to hand out at the office dinner or party. Many houses, schools, banks, and stores will provide a table or a corner for a *pesebre* (nativity scene), which can be quite elaborate. After workers collect their Christmas bonuses a great exodus takes place as people travel from the cities to their hometowns. Business activity begins to wrap up from December 15 to 18 until the schools open again after January 6.

On Christmas Eve, families assemble for dinner at about 10:00 p.m. Traditional for this meal are *hallacas* (corn-dough parcels with a filling, wrapped in a plantain leaf), *ensalada de gallina* (shredded chicken, diced potatoes, peas, and mayonnaise), *pernil* (roast shoulder of ham), and *pan de jamon* (a long, thin bread with ham and raisins inside). Sparkling wine, whiskey, or beer may be drunk, but the traditional festive tipple is *ponche crema,* a creamy blend of condensed milk with rum or brandy served in small glasses, like eggnog.

Midnight is greeted with noisy fireworks and general merrymaking as adults exchange gifts around the Christmas tree and children receive their presents from El Niño Jesús. Many people will attend the Misa de Gallo (Midnight Mass) in the local church, where *aguinaldos* (hymns) are sung.

Christmas Day is not a big deal for most families. Stores are closed, and people either stay at home with the family or visit friends and relatives.

THE HALLACA

The most important dish at Christmas is without doubt the *hallaca* (pronounced "eye-ya-ka"), a cornmeal-dough pocket stuffed with tasty ingredients, wrapped in a plantain leaf, and boiled. Similar to the *tamales* and *humitas* served in other parts of Latin America, the *hallaca* is eaten only at Christmas, and has pride of place on the Christmas dinner plate.

The exact origin of the *hallaca* is not known, but it is believed to come from the custom of plantation owners giving their slaves the leftovers from their Christmas banquets. The slaves would add these scraps to the boiled cornmeal dough (known as *bollos*) that made up their daily diet. That is why *hallacas* are stuffed with such an odd range of things, from chicken, beef, and pork stew to olives, raisins, capers, and even boiled eggs, depending on the family recipe.

Making *hallacas* is an elaborate process with many stages, and in Venezuela usually involves the whole family, who will spend a weekend  making enough *hallacas* to last a month, each one wrapped in a leaf and tied with string, like a little present.

Año Nuevo (New Year's Eve. December 31)
New Year traditions in Venezuela involve various ways of saying good-bye to the old year and

welcoming the new one in a way that will bring good luck, good health, love, and prosperity. Sold by street vendors and smart lingerie stores alike, yellow underwear (the color of gold) is worn by both men and women to bring luck and money in the year to come. Red pants are believed to improve your chances at finding love and romance. Another popular custom is to wear new clothes—known as *estrenos*—to start the year well dressed.

New Year's Eve parties follow the same pattern as Christmas Eve, with a late meal of traditional Christmas food, and dancing to festive music such as *gaitas,* salsa, and reggaeton. Typical New Year tunes are "Viejo Año" by Maracaibo 15, Nestor Zavarce's tearjerker "Faltan Cinco Pa' Las Doce" ("Five Minutes to Twelve"), and "Año Nuevo, Vida Nueva" ("New Year, New Life") by Billo's Caracas Boys.

Just before midnight everybody takes twelve grapes and a glass of sparkling wine. The idea is to gobble down a grape for each of the twelve chimes, with each grape representing a good month in the year to come. The last chime of midnight ends with the deafening sound of *los cañonazos*—the fireworks that mark the start of the New Year, and hugs and kisses all round.

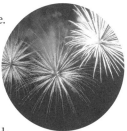

In the Andean states of Mérida and Tachira they say good-bye to the old year by parading papier-maché figures through the streets and burning them at midnight, to the sound of *gaita* music and the deafening explosions of thousands of *triquitraquis* (firecrackers).

Carnaval (Carnival. Four days before Lent)

Venezuela has nothing to rival the world-famous carnival celebrations in Brazil, but many towns have street parties and parades. In Caracas there are small parades for children in fancy dress, but the biggest celebrations are held in Carúpano, where floats with sound systems and followers in carnival costumes do circuits of the town.

The most distinct celebration is in El Callao, Bolívar State, where West Indian and Antillean immigrants arriving in an 1880s gold rush brought calypso, which is still sung in English. Popular carnival characters in El Callao include women in African-style head scarves and dresses reminiscent of nineteenth-century Guadeloupe called Las Madamas; masked *diablos* (devils) with tridents and tails who keep the crowds in check; and the *mediopintos*—men and women with black paint who threaten to splash it over you if you don't pay them.

In Mérida, Carnival coincides with the ten-day Feria del Sol, which features concerts, beauty pageants, and bullfights.

Semana Santa (Holy Week/Easter)

A movable feast in the Catholic Church celebrating the crucifixion and resurrection of Jesus Christ, Semana Santa falls in March/April. It starts with Domingo de Ramos (Palm Sunday) and concludes with Domingo de Resurrección (Easter Sunday).

In Caracas the festivities begin with the blessing of palm leaves brought down from the Ávila Mountain by the Palmeros de Chacao. This tradition dates back to 1770, when the population of Caracas was decimated by a deadly outbreak of yellow fever. A local priest, José Antonio García Mohedano, made a promise to God that he would send men to cut palms on the Ávila every year if the fever stopped. Ever since then it has been a tradition among local families to pledge to cut palms for five, ten, or twenty years.

Colorful processions of people dressed in long purple robes take place in many cities and towns across the country on the evening of Holy Wednesday, when churches parade statues of Christ carrying the cross. On Viernes Santo (Good Friday) there are passion plays around the Stations of the Cross, with devotees dressing as Roman soldiers, the Virgin Mary, and Christ. A very realistic crucifixion scene is reenacted in Tostós in Trujillo State and in many villages around Mérida. Easter celebrations end on Sunday with the *Quema de Judas* (burning of Judas), in which papier-maché effigies of unpopular local figures or politicians are dressed in old clothes and publicly burned.

Corpus Christi (Ninth Thursday after Holy Thursday)
Spectacular festivals of masked *diablos danzantes* (devil dancers) take place in fourteen Venezuelan

towns and villages in a centuries-old tradition brought from Spain and adapted to express the defiance of the African slaves, who were barred from entering church during Sunday mass. From sunrise the devils parade through town, causing mischief, mayhem, and general devilment until about midday, when they make a mock attack on the church. They are repelled by the priest, who holds aloft the consecrated hosts of the Eucharist. Three times the devils attack, and three times they are repelled. Finally, with good having triumphed over evil, the devils remove their masks and the street parties begin in earnest.

The most celebrated devil dancers are in San Francisco de Yare, which is near Caracas in the Valles del Tuy. Dressed from head to foot in red, the Yare devils carry maracas and wear multicolored horned masks made from papier-maché. In the coastal cacao plantation of Chuao, famous for its high-quality cocoa beans, isolation has helped to preserve many traditional elements of devil dancing, including costumes made of colored rags.

San Juan Bautista (St. John the Baptist. June 23, 24)

The feast of St. John the Baptist is celebrated in dramatic style with three days of Afro-Venezuelan *tambores* (drums) and call-and-response singing accompanied by vibrant dancing in which men and women circle closely around each other in fast, hip-swiveling movements that grow more suggestive as the night wears on.

Statues of the saint as a baby or child are dressed in red or blue and bathed in rum, before being

paraded by flag-waving crowds through the towns of
Curiepe and Birongo, and the coastal villages of
Cuyagua, Choroní, Chuao, and Chuspa.

In some coastal towns the local fishermen take
their local San Juan statue out to sea to meet those
from other towns, then head back to land for an
extended party.

FOLKLORE AND SUPERSTITIONS

Many popular beliefs and superstitions in Venezuela
are linked to Catholic beliefs, especially the idea that
you can make a pact with a saint or holy figure for
help with an earthly problem that needs divine
intervention. The person making the request must
promise to do something in return and carry it out,
which is known as *pagando promesa.* This is the
driving force behind the *diablos danzantes,* who do
not dance each year simply to keep an old tradition
alive but instead make a solemn promise in front
of the church to dance for a number of years.

For example, San Antonio, it is believed, can help
you to find love if his statue is suspended upside
down; or if you regularly light a candle and say a
prayer in front of the image of San Onofre, it is said
that he will help you to get a job or pass an exam.

The most popular of these folk saints is Dr. José
Gregorio Hernández, a Venezuelan doctor who was
killed in a car crash in 1919 and has been declared
"venerable" by the Catholic Church. Although he is
not officially a Catholic saint, there is great devotion
to the good doctor. His tomb in the church of La
Candelaria, Caracas, and his birthplace in Isnotú,
Trujillo State, are popular places of pilgrimage,

especially by the sick and infirm seeking a miracle cure. Known as "the doctor of the poor," he is depicted wearing a black suit and hat with a Charlie Chaplin moustache, or in a doctor's white coat.

An indication of the importance of magic in the lives of many Venezuelans is the number of stores known as *perfumerías* in most towns and villages. Offering tobacco readings and spiritual healing, they sell a dizzying array of soaps for washing away bad luck and love potions to make you irresistible, alongside shelves of saints, Buddhas, and strange paraphernalia for practicing *brujería* (witchcraft).

The Cult of María Lionza

A uniquely Venezuelan blend of folk Catholicism and African and indigenous ritual, the mysterious and magical cult of María Lionza began in the mountains of Sorte in Yaracuy State, but became a countrywide phenomenon with the move to the big cities in the 1940s and '50s. The closest parallels in Latin America are with Cuban santeria or Haitian voodoo.

Pilgrims come most weekends to carry out rituals in the forests of Sorte, with mediums in a trancelike state channeling the spirits of religious, mythical, and historical figures, such as Dr. José Gregorio Hernández, Simón Bolívar, and even a group of Vikings. At the top of this pantheon is a group

The Myth of María Lionza

María Lionza, or Yara, was an indigenous princess, the daughter of Yaracuy, chief of the Nivar tribe. Before her birth the shaman had pronounced that, if a girl with strange, watery-green eyes were born, she would have to be sacrificed and offered to the Great Anaconda, or she would bring death and destruction to the tribe. The chief, unable to sacrifice his daughter, hid her in a mountain cave with twenty-two warriors to guard her.

One day, while the guards were asleep, Yara left the cave and walked to a lagoon where she saw her reflection for the first time. Captivated by her own image, she was unable to move, but her presence awakened the Great Anaconda, who instantly fell in love with her. When she resisted its advances the anaconda swallowed the girl, but immediately began to swell up, forcing water out of the lagoon, flooding the village, and drowning the whole tribe. Finally, the anaconda burst and María Lionza was set free, becoming the protector of lakes, rivers, and all living things.

known as the *Tres Potencias* (Three Powers): María Lionza, depicted as a queen with a crown; the black independence fighter Negro Felipe, and the Indian chief Guaicaipuro.

Rituals are carried out to the sounds of Afro-Venezuelan drums and crowds who chant "*Fuerza, fuerza*" (strength, strength) to encourage the entranced mediums. On days special to the cult, such as October 12, the noise can be overwhelming.

Nobody knows the true origin of the cult, or of María Lionza herself, who is sometimes called Yara, or *La Reina* (the Queen). Some images and statues show her as a European woman with a golden crown, others as an Indian princess living wild in nature. The famous statue in Caracas from the 1950s depicts her as a naked woman sitting astride a tapir, holding a human pelvis in her raised arms.

TRADITIONAL MUSIC AND DANCE

Venezuela has a rich tradition of folk music that combines indigenous, European, and African elements.

Joropo, or *música llanera*, is a musical style from Los Llanos and the most popular folk music in Venezuela. It is played wherever beef is being barbecued, and competes with salsa and merengue on many small buses. It is traditionally sung in a rough, nasal style by cowboy types in Stetsons and pointed boots, with music provided by a thirty-two-string harp, a *cuatro* (a small, four-stringed guitar), and maracas. *Joropo* evolved from the *zarzuelas* and *cante jondo* brought to Venezuela by the Spanish, and the jaunty pace of the music is said to evoke the galloping hoofs of a wild horse. *Joropo* is also a dance, a sort of waltz involving jerky, cucaracha-stomping steps by the man, known as *zapateo*, and dizzy twirls by his female partner.

Simón Díaz and Reynaldo Armas are perhaps Venezuela's best-loved *llanero* singers, although legendary performers like Juan Vicente Torrealba, Ignacio "El Indio" Figueredo, and El Carrao de Palmarito are still played regularly on the radio. Talented young harpists include Leonard Jacome, who has experimented with *joropo*-jazz fusion, and Carlos Orozco, nicknamed "Metralleta" (machine gun) for his dazzling finger play. Every year festivals are held in Venezuela and Colombia, with prizes for the best singers, harpists, and dancers, and tests of lyrical skill called *contrapunteo*, when contestants try to outdo each other by inventing rhymes on the spot in a head-to-head battle.

If *joropo* is the music of the plains, then Afro-Venezuelan music called *tambores* (drums) is the sound of the beach. Harking backs to slave days, *tambores* is still played in the old plantation towns along the central coast, such as Choroni, Chuao, Puerto Maya, and the beach towns of Barlovento. Played fast and loud on long *cumaco* drums made from hollowed-out avocado tree trunks, *tambores* preserves West African polyrhythms, with one drummer playing a deer or cowhide skin on the front of the drum and two or more playing on the trunk with hard sticks called *palillos*. This is what gives the music the distinctive "taca-ta-taca-ta" sound that drives the dancing, which takes place in a circle formed by the *cantor* (singer) and the chorus.

One man and one woman dance together at any one time, the man trying to get as close as possible as he circles around her, shaking his hips, while she fends off his advances by spinning away from him. Other dancers can cut in at any time, and the dancing continues until the drummers give up or the rum runs out. During Cruz de Mayo (May Cross, held on May 3) celebrations there is no dancing to *tambores,* as the songs to the cross are more religious in nature.

The other main folk music style is the *gaitas* music of Zulia, which is usually heard only at Christmas, although in Maracaibo it is played all year. *Gaitas* is Spanish for bagpipes, but there are no bagpipes in Venezuelan *gaitas* music, which is played on *cuatro*, maracas, and the odd-looking *furruco*, a drum with a stick attached, played by rubbing the stick, which makes a very distinctive sound. Modern *gaitas* is played on electric keyboard and bass guitar by groups such as Guaco and Maracaibo 15, and competes with salsa and merengue at parties and discos in the run-up to Christmas.

SIMÓN DÍAZ—VENEZUELAN FOLK LEGEND

Tío Simón (Uncle Simon), as he is known to his fans, is considered a national treasure in Venezuela. For many years he hosted a children's show that promoted folk traditions, humor, and songs. Born on August 8, 1928, in Barbacoas, Guarico State, he is famous for his renditions of folk songs known collectively as *joropo*. His most famous composition is "Caballo Viejo" ("Old Horse"), which became a huge international hit for the Franco-Spanish group the Gipsy Kings after they renamed the song "Bamboleo." He also recorded a very popular version of the country's unofficial anthem "Alma Llanera" ("Llanos Soul").

Over a career spanning more than sixty years, he singlehandedly rescued for future generations the traditional working songs of the Llanos called *tonadas,* reinterpreting them with spare arrangements that bring to life the daily chores of the cattle ranch.

chapter four

THE VENEZUELANS AT HOME

Venezuela is a vast country, but its population is very unevenly spread, with more than 90 percent living in urban environments, and 80 percent in the five largest cities. The mass migration from the countryside to the urban centers began in the late 1940s as investment shifted away from traditional exports of plantation crops like coffee, sugar, and cocoa to the rapidly expanding oil industry.

Oil earnings were used by the dictator Marcos Pérez Jiménez to finance an ambitious program of public works that saw Caracas transformed from

Fairy Tale of Caracas

For many foreigners arriving in Venezuela, their first experience of the country is seeing the flickering lights on the hillsides as they are driven up the highway from Maiquetia airport to Caracas. "How quaint is that?" a friend once said, "It looks like a little nativity scene with those fairy lights twinkling on the mountainside." The reality set in the next day, when we drove back down to the beach and my friend saw the red cinder blocks and zinc roofs of the shantytowns, the upper stories of the rickety *ranchos* so close they nearly touch, and the spaghetti-tangle of electricity and phone cables strung out between them. The "fairy lights" of the night before were the bare bulbs that illuminate the narrow streets and crumbling concrete steps that run up and down the hillside like a surreal image by M. C. Escher—but for the poor in Caracas the image is all too real.

the "city of red roofs," as it was known, to a concrete metropolis designed for cars and vertical living. Work on constructing the new highways, hotels, overpasses, and sports stadiums attracted both rural migrants from the interior and foreign immigrants from Spain and Italy, who came to start a new life in a land of opportunity. However, mass migration also saw the rise of the slums, most of which were well established in Caracas and other cities by the 1960s.

Where you live in Venezuela, and your family background, still has an impact on daily life. Life in the city is very different from life in the countryside, and there is a great difference between rich and poor. In 2010 President Chávez hailed a report by the Economic Commission for Latin America and the Caribbean (ECLAC) that stated that Venezuela had reduced extreme poverty from 27 percent in 1999 to 7 percent. But, despite government attempts to tackle poverty and increase access to education, medical care, and subsidized groceries, a huge wealth gap still remains.

HOUSING

Venezuelans live in all sorts of houses, from the Beverly Hills–type mansions of the mega-rich, who live in gated communities, to the high-rise apartment blocks of the middle classes, and the straw *shabono* dwellings of the Yanomami Indians deep in the rain forest. Wherever they live, whether in mansions or cinder-block shacks, Venezuelans are united by a love of family, especially children, a desire to improve their lot, and an optimism for the future.

Pressure on urban space in a country where so many people live in cities has led to vertical solutions in city centers, where high-rise buildings are the norm, and satellite towns of two-story houses for middle- and working-class commuters.

Some traditional colonial housing does exist, notably in the city of Coro, which was founded in 1527 and is one of the oldest towns in Venezuela. A UN World Heritage Site, it has well-preserved adobe-walled houses built around central open courtyards, often with a mango or papaya tree for shade. In Caracas, there are a number of important colonial houses around Plaza Bolívar, including the nearby house in which Simón Bolívar was born. The best-preserved eighteenth-century house in Caracas is the Quinta Anauco.

On a more modest scale, in the countryside and along the coast, many small towns and fishing villages have colonial-style buildings, one-story houses with small windows, concrete or packed-earth floors, and an open courtyard at the back to take advantage of the breeze and keep the house cool.

When Venezuelans talk about "*la gente del cerro*" (the people on the hillside), they aren't referring to the privileged inhabitants of luxury hillside apartments, who live far from the traffic, noise, and overcrowding of downtown Caracas. The hills where expensive apartment buildings with security guards are located are called *lomas*. The *cerros* are the sprawling shantytowns built by poor people with their own hands that cling precariously to the hillsides surrounding the valley and provide shelter for some 50 percent of the city's residents.

Roughly half of all urban dwellers live in unplanned shantytowns, or *barrios*. Some *barrios* are enormous. The Jose Felix Ribas *barrio*, in the east of Caracas, is considered one of the largest shantytowns in Latin America, home to an estimated 120,000 people crammed into 237 acres. Only the Ávila Mountain that separates Caracas from the Caribbean Sea—declared a national park in 1958—has managed to escape the encroachment of *ranchos*—cinder-block shacks with zinc roofs.

Most established *barrios* have access to gas, water, and electricity, but in some of the newest settlements on the highest slopes residents of the *ranchos* have no running water or sewage facilities. They have to hook up to the electricity grid illegally and bring fresh water up—or garbage down—the steep concrete steps that interconnect the streets of the *barrio* with the city below.

A major consequence of living where cars can't pass and where the police are sometimes afraid to go is that crime is rampant in poorer areas and many people are afraid to leave their houses after dark. A large percentage of the weekend death toll

can be traced to the *barrios* and the young gangs of
malandros (thugs) and drug dealers who fight it out
with guns for dominance of the streets.

FAMILY LIFE

Family life is built around the home and the extended
family. As we have seen, elderly relatives stay with
their families rather than go into old people's homes,
and young adults remain at home for some years.

Children are doted upon. Some visitors react with
terror when strangers come up and touch their
children in the street, or make comments like, "*Tu
niña es tan linda quiero comerla a besos*" ("Your child
is so pretty, I want to eat her up with kisses"), but
Venezuelans are used to it, growing up in large
families with young children and babies around.

A WAY WITH NAMES

Some Venezuelans like to invent unique
names for their children. They may combine
their own names to create hybrids like Nelmar
(Nelson and María), or reverse a name to get
Susej (Jesús) or Aseret (Teresa). Anglo-Saxon
names assume strange spellings, such as
Jhon, Jhonni, Chirly (Shirley), and Yeferson
(Jefferson). There was a fad in the 1960s
and '70s for political names such as Stalin,
Maolenin, and Hochemin. Popular names
today are Leididi, a tribute to Diana, Princess
of Wales, and Maickolyakson. Yesaidú is a
girl's name taken from the English "yes I do."

Life can be a real struggle for poorer families, which generally have more mouths to feed and a greater reliance on public rather than expensive private health care. A macho attitude prevails among some men who believe the number of children they have is a sign of their virility. A failure to take on responsibility for the children they father with multiple partners means that much child rearing in poor and rural areas is done by single women with the help of their family. If a woman can't cope with a child, or if a child is orphaned, it is not unusual for it to be brought up by a grandmother or aunt.

High inflation and rising costs means that many poorer women are forced to work two jobs to make ends meet—a situation known as "*matando tigre*" (killing a tiger)—or work in the informal economy selling sweets and cakes or setting up street stalls. Some children have to work shining shoes or looking after parked cars to raise extra cash for the family.

That doesn't mean Venezuelans aren't generous. Even the poorest family will invite a visitor in for coffee and a bite to eat. A popular saying is "*Donde comen dos comen tres*," which means that if there's food for two there's food for three.

For both rich and poor, family life revolves around holidays and family celebrations. There are plenty of occasions for Venezuelans to let their hair down, forget the bad times, crack a smile, and party like there's no tomorrow.

HOME HELP
Wealthy and upper-middle-class families generally have one or more servants living in the house to

clean, cook, make beds, look after the children, and do the shopping. They may also have a gardener, a chauffeur, and a security guard. The number of servants in a house is seen as an indication of status.

Live-in maids typically have to wear a uniform provided by their employer, and are given a strict roster of chores. The word *cachifa* will often be heard in Venezuela to describe a live-in maid, although it is considered impolite to use in front of a maid.

A recurring story line in Venezuelan soap operas is the rags-to-riches tale of a maid who falls in love with her employer's son and, after many trials and tribulations, becomes the lady of the house. This rather romantic view of life, which is pitched at maids having a post-lunch break while their employers enjoy a siesta, is far from the reality. Most women in service earn very little money, sleep in a small room off the kitchen, and have limited contact with their families—including their children—who might live miles away in the countryside.

Servants who have lived with their employers for many years may be treated as part of the family and live-in nannies often establish strong bonds with the children they care for that blur the usual divisions between family and servant.

Among the middle and professional classes it is typical for women with high-powered jobs to have some kind of home help, but they are more likely to employ a house cleaner for a few days a week than have a live-in maid. Contracting cleaners or nannies is generally done through personal recommendation or through an agency, due to security fears.

It is quite common even for poor families to pay somebody from the neighborhood to come in and look after the children or help with washing and cooking on an ad hoc basis. This reflects the lack of employment opportunities and low wages for many Venezuelans.

DAILY LIFE

Venezuelans often travel far to work or study, and weekdays can start early, at about 5:00 a.m. *Desayuno* (breakfast) is usually an *arepa* with scrambled eggs or ham and cheese, or a bowl of cereal, and coffee. Those in a rush will grab a quick snack from a bakery, and wash it down with fruit juice or coffee. Children will walk or take a bus or the Metro to school, starting early because of the heat. Commuters from the satellite towns around Caracas have to start especially early to beat the traffic.

Offices open at about 7:00 or 8:00 a.m., and there is usually a coffee machine or a nearby kiosk or bakery for a mid-morning break. Lunch is taken in the two hours between midday and 2:00 p.m., and is usually an hour long, although people stretch it to two hours when they can. The siesta is rare these days in Venezuela, so the days of the long *almuerzo* (lunch) are over, and heavy traffic makes it hard for people to get home for a meal. Most workers will bring a home-made meal, or go out for pasta or *pabellon criollo* at one of the cheap restaurants offering a *menú ejecutivo* or *menú del día*, where you get a two-course meal an a drink for a fixed price.

In some places, however, especially in laid-back rural areas, shops might close until 3:00 p.m. for a siesta. Offices close at about 6:00 p.m., and many people have coffee or a drink with colleagues or do some shopping before heading home to avoid the worst of the rush hour traffic.

The evening meal (*cena*) is usually at home, with the whole family seated at the table, and is generally taken between 7:00 and 9.00 p.m. It will probably consist of soup followed by a main course of meat, chicken, or fish with rice, black beans, or mashed potato, and a side of salad.

EVERYDAY SHOPPING

Even if they live in big cities, Venezuelans will do their shopping as if they lived in a small town, buying groceries in little stores close to home and building a personal relationship with local shopkeepers. Most groceries can be found in the local *abasto,* the equivalent of a mom-and-pop shop and typically run by Portuguese owners. Every town and village in Venezuela, no matter how small, will have at least one *abasto*, *licorería* (liquor store), and *farmacia* (pharmacy). The other important stop on the daily shopping trip is the *panadería* (bakery), which not only sells *canillas* (baguettes) but is a good place to have coffee and a chat and buy cold cuts and cheese from the deli counter.

This concept of "buying local" extends to the *barrios*, where many homes sell sweets, cakes, savory snacks, or beer from the front windows of their houses to earn some extra cash. When the alternative of visiting the local *abasto*

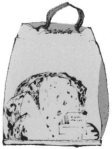

involves a long walk up and down steep steps, paying a few BsF more for essentials makes sense.

Another aspect of the informal economy is the selling of fruit and vegetables on the street from trucks that come direct from the countryside. These compete with the many street vendors who set up stalls selling everything from fresh food to clothes, and established markets, where prices might be higher. Pirated CDs and DVDs are also sold on the street for a fraction of the store prices.

There are several large chain supermarkets that stock all the usual things you would find in the USA or the UK. A recent phenomenon, the Mercales are government-subsidized shops that sell basic foods at discounted prices. Some have blamed these for distorting the market, undercutting private stores, and leading to shortages of some basics, such as coffee, powdered milk, beef, and chicken. When faced with a shortage of an essential item, Venezuelan housewives travel from store to store until they find it, leading to long lines in some supermarkets as word spreads.

The other major shopping destinations are the mega-malls found in the big cities, like the Sambil chain of shopping centers, where people go to window-shop and hang out as much as to buy clothes and gadgets.

MARRIAGE, DIVORCE, AND *CONCUBINATO*

There are few festive occasions in Venezuela as joyous as a wedding. Guests dress up in their best, and the couple, best man, and bridesmaids wear rented tuxedos and dresses. The ceremony takes place in the cool of the evening, and is followed by canapés or a buffet, and dancing to a live band or DJ.

Well-off couples will go whole hog and have an extravagant church wedding and reception, and post their photographs in the society pages of the newspapers. Less lavish celebrations are the norm for those with more modest resources, but three things you can always expect at a Venezuelan wedding are the rice that guests throw over the happy couple, the whiskey served at the reception, and the *hora loca* (crazy hour), when hats and masks are handed out to

guests at midnight and the dancing starts in earnest.

Civil ceremonies are held in front of a justice of the peace and can take place in the register offices or at home. Many Venezuelans decorate their house or apartment, invite their friends, and have a party after saying their vows and signing the register.

Divorce has been legal since 1909, and is not a complicated process.

Although a Catholic country, Venezuela has quite high rates of *concubinato* (consensual union), particularly in rural areas and inner city *barrios*, in which couples live together as husband and wife without going through a civil or church wedding. Some go on to tie the knot in a civil ceremony, but many do not. As children are given both paternal and maternal surnames, there is no real stigma in being the offspring of a consensual union. Once registered, these relationships have the status of civil partnerships under the law.

EDUCATION

Venezuela has a system of free education open to all, and a parallel system of fee-paying private schools and colleges.

School attendance is compulsory from the age of six to seventeen years. Although some children start their education in private institutions, the majority start at a *preescolar* (pre-school) between the ages of three and six. *Primaria* (primary school) is from age six to twelve, and S*ecundaria* (high school) up to seventeen. The last year of high school is called *Quinto Año*, when students have the chance to take the *Bachillerato* (Baccalaureate).

A recent campaign by the government, called Misión Robinson, has had great success in virtually eradicating adult illiteracy, which stood at 11 percent of the population in 1992. As part of the program, teachers were dispatched all over the country, including to remote indigenous communities, and more than a million adults learned to read and write between 2003 and 2005. Misión Ribas is another government program that gives adults who never

finished high school the chance to gain their high school certificates and apply for university admission.

There are more than thirty-two universities and more than ninety technical institutes. Women take up 52 percent of university enrollment.

The oldest and largest public university is the Universidad Central de Venezuela (UCV), which occupies a huge campus in the center of Caracas and teaches about 58,000 students. It was designed by Venezuelan architect Carlos Raúl Villanueva between 1944 and 1960. Recognized as a masterpiece of modernist architecture, it is a UNESCO World Heritage Site. Murals and sculptures by Alexander Calder are dotted around the campus.

The other major university is the Universidad de los Andes in Mérida, which dates back to 1810 and has some 40,000 students.

LEISURE

Living in crowded *barrios*, dealing with gridlocked traffic, and holding sometimes two or more jobs to make ends meet, Venezuelan city dwellers love to head for the park or the beach on weekends.

Parks

Parks are the perfect places for families to hang up a papier-maché piñata to celebrate a child's birthday, cook some meat on a barbecue, and enjoy some fresh air. They are also perfect for practicing sports, and you'll find softball teams, joggers, judo classes, and yoga groups taking full advantage of the space,

alongside young lovers who live at home and need somewhere to hold hands and smooch.

You can spend all day in some Caracas parks, like Parque Generalísimo Francisco de Miranda in Altamira, which has an acoustic shell for concerts, a mini-zoo of tropical birds and animals, a boating lake, and a re-creation of Christopher Columbus's ship *La Santa María*.

Beaches
The beach is another typical weekend destination for many Venezuelans, as so many people live in the cities near the coast. Venezuelans will usually travel to the beach en masse, with extended family or large groups of friends taking food, drinks, and music along to give a day at the beach a party atmosphere.

Mountain Hikes
In Caracas, the middle classes will be found walking the mountain trail from Altamira up to the ranger

station at Sabas Nieves on Cerro El Ávila, the impressive mountain that separates the city from the Caribbean Sea and dominates the skyline. An extension of the Andes, the Ávila rises to a height of 8,990 ft (2,740 meters) at Pico Naiguata, its highest point. Declared a national park in 1958 to stop the encroachment of slum dwellings and preserve the forest, the Ávila is known as "the lungs of Caracas." The trail to Sabas Nieves is a place for the city's beautiful people to see and be seen, and some hikers dress to impress in spandex and full makeup.

Cable Car

Those who can't make the three-hour trek to the top of the mountain take the cable car for fifteen minutes up to the spectacular Humboldt Hotel—a pet project of the dictator Marcos Pérez Jimenez in the 1950s. The area around the hotel offers cool respite from the heat of the valley, magnificent views of the sea, and stalls selling blackberries and other fruits grown on the mountain slopes of Galipan.

Shopping Malls

The other great leisure pursuit in the cities is spending a day at one of the massive shopping malls, such as the Sambil in Caracas, where you can shop or window-shop, eat a snack or a full meal at a range of local and US franchises, have a few beers, watch a game at a sports bar, and take in a movie at the multiplex.

The main draw of the shopping malls is that they allow people of all social classes to hang out in a safe environment. That's an important benefit in a country where insecurity is a big factor in determining where you feel safe to go and where you don't.

chapter five

MAKING FRIENDS

Venezuelans are naturally friendly people who like nothing more than gathering together in groups to drink, dance, swap stories, and have fun. With big extended families the norm, and socializing a way of life, Venezuelans generally have an inner circle of friends made up of cousins, neighbors, and high school or university buddies, and an outer circle of work colleagues and other acquaintances.

This is different from the norm in the USA or northern Europe, where family ties are not generally as strong and people form their main circle of friends at school or at work. What it means in practical terms is that foreigners will find Venezuelans will readily include them in group or after-work activities, but making the extra step into the inner circle of trusted friends and being invited home to meet the family generally takes longer, and is therefore a significant honor if it happens.

The biggest problem facing a foreigner in Venezuela is the language barrier. If you don't speak Spanish you will be limited to very basic communication. While this will not deter Venezuelans from including you in social events, or trying to make jokes, or showing you how to dance, it will make it harder to get to know people.

FIRST CONTACT

As we have seen, Venezuelans are always up for a friendly chat. They enjoy meeting foreigners and, given a chance, like to teach them something about their country and culture. Your first contacts are usually with the taxi driver taking you to your hotel, the receptionist booking you in, and the waiter serving you your first Polar beer. Use these opportunities to try out your Spanish, and engage with the Venezuelans you meet with all the Spanish you can muster.

However, be wary of people who come up to you in the street or on the beach with a line like, "Hey, friend, where you from?" At best, they are hustlers looking to make a buck out of a tourist, and at worst, they are scam artists or thieves. They will probably offer to show you around, or take you to the best place to change money; you'll end up paying one way or another. The trick is not to get hooked in the first place, by avoiding eye contact and ignoring unwanted attempts to attract your attention in the street, as a Venezuelan would. If you do find you've picked up an unwanted companion, a polite "*No quiero nada, gracias*" (I don't want anything, thanks) and a wave of the hand should end the matter, but if they insist, be firm and walk away, or enter a store or restaurant, as you'll never get rid of them otherwise.

MEETING VENEZUELANS

If your Spanish is basic, it will be hard to start up conversations, but you will be able to find Venezuelans who speak English, mainly among the foreign-educated elite, but also in firms that have business dealings with the USA or the UK, and in the tourism industry. Hotel staff and tour guides especially will be happy to speak to you and practice their English. Use the opportunity to pick up some Spanish from them.

If you speak Spanish reasonably well you will find it much easier to meet Venezuelans everywhere you go, whether you're in the country on business or as a tourist. If you are working in Venezuela then you will soon find that the social side of office life involves birthday cakes and trips out to lunch with colleagues. These are the first steps to making friends, so take every opportunity that presents itself.

Venezuelan friendships are made up of close groups, so if you are invited to meet the other members of somebody's social circle it's a good sign that you have made a positive impression. Your own circle of friends will start to grow. Be careful not to snub somebody by turning down an invitation to share time with colleagues and new acquaintances, as you could give the impression that you don't want to make friends and find no further invitations coming your way. Venezuelans have specific expressions like *rompe grupo* (group breaker) and *aguafiestas* (killjoy) to describe people they don't want at a party.

CONVERSATION STARTERS AND STOPPERS

It's important to remember that Venezuelans are people-pleasers and spend a lot of time on social niceties and flattery. They like light conversations that make them smile. They don't like talk that reminds them of their daily difficulties or criticizes their country.

Typically, they'll start with how nice it is to see you, and ask questions about your family and, particularly with foreigners, about your experience of Venezuela. They will be genuinely interested in your comments about their country, but it is best to stick to positive impressions about the friendly people, the lovely weather, the beautiful beaches, and the tasty food. Any criticisms should be reserved for conversations with Venezuelans you know well enough to engage in a serious debate.

This is not because Venezuelans don't like to hear criticism of their country, or don't debate the big issues of the day. They do—you'll hear plenty of people moaning about the political situation, the traffic, and the rising cost of living, among other things. However, a foreigner wading in with a list of all the country's failings runs the risk of upsetting people and sounding arrogant. The word for somebody negative is *antipático*. If you want to make friends you have to be seen as *simpático* (nice). This is an issue of pride and respect. While it may be acceptable for members of a family to criticize a brother or sister within the group, they will steadfastly defend the same brother or sister against any criticism from outside .

The same goes for discussions about the political situation. Given the polarized nature of the country, any comments about President Chávez, good or bad, risk upsetting somebody in the group. That's why Venezuelans will go out of their way to avoid talking politics. It's much better to stick to less divisive topics, such as sports, music, or soap opera story lines, and ask questions about the best places to visit, the best beer to drink, and the best restaurants in town.

INVITATIONS HOME

With work associates you might find that most, if not all, of your social encounters take place at bars and restaurants in the evenings, and in parks or at the beach on weekends. Unless you're in a relationship, and your partner asks you home to meet the folks, it is rare to break into that inner circle and be invited to somebody's house.

One factor of this is that the home is a family space, and extended families will often live under the same roof, sometimes making it difficult to have outsiders over. But there is also an issue of class. Poorer Venezuelans will live in *barrios,* where they are used to neighbors and friends they have grown up with popping in unannounced. While no birthday or christening goes uncelebrated in the close-knit community of a *barrio*, some people will be self-conscious about inviting somebody from outside the *barrio* to their neighborhood. They will have a small celebration at work with colleagues as well.

Most upper- and middle-class Venezuelans will have their own house or apartment and will be more used to hosting dinner parties for friends. The etiquette is simple: never arrive early or on time, as nobody will be expecting you yet, so be about twenty minutes late; always bring something to drink, such as beer, wine, or a good whiskey; and come prepared to dance, even if the invitation is for dinner.

CLUBS AND ASSOCIATIONS

As a stepping-stone into Venezuelan society, visitors coming to the country for any length of time might like to seek out some of the expatriate groups that meet up in the major cities. It's best to avoid getting stuck in an expatriate bubble, but members of these groups will help you to meet Venezuelans. Your local embassy is a good place to start investigating such groups, but you can also get in touch with business associations like the Cámara Venezolano Americana de Comercio e Industria (Venamcham) or the Cámara Venezolano Británica de Comercio (CVBC, or Britcham).

In Caracas, there is a well-attended Hash House Harriers group, which meets regularly for a fun run and drinks.

SOCIALIZING WITH THE OPPOSITE SEX

Working out the rules of the dating game in Venezuela can be very confusing for foreigners from the USA and northern Europe, but it is essential to learn the basic ground rules if you want to link up with a member of the opposite sex.

The first thing to understand is that Venezuelan men and women are very comfortable socializing with each other. Growing up in large family groups, with regular excuses for parties and get-togethers, there are no awkward divisions between boys and girls or old and young.

Be aware that an invitation to dance is not seen as a romantic or sexual gesture, despite the stereotypes you sometimes see in northern Europe or the USA of salsa as "sex standing up." People can dance very close together to salsa and merengue without any sexual connotations. Dancing is a natural part of any social event in Venezuela. The ease with which all generations of an extended family or group of friends will dance together means there are few wallflowers.

This familiarity and ease with the opposite sex extends to male and female work friends, who will happily go in a group for an after-work drink or meal, or even for a weekend at the beach, with no implications of anything but good clean friendly fun.

Venezuelans are also very flattering and complimentary to friends and associates. Men might find that women will often ask them quite intimate questions about their current romantic situation and past relationships, which can come across as flirty, but should not be misconstrued as an indication of romantic interest. Venezuelan men in particular can be very chivalrous, smiling, complimenting a woman on her appearance, and calling her *mi cielo* (my heaven), *mi reina* (my queen), *mi amorcito* (my little love), or *mi cosita preciosa* (my sweet little thing), just as a normal part of saying hello. This could constitute a pick-up strategy, but you shouldn't jump to conclusions or take offense just because a Venezuelan man spouts a few flowery phrases. He probably does it to everybody.

On the street, however, women, especially the blonde and blue-eyed, who attract more male attention, can expect to hear unwelcome comments from strangers. These usually start with a "*psst, psst*" or a "*mamacita*" ("little mommy") to get your attention and continue with a line about how beautiful you are, and how God must be crying because one of his angels has fallen from heaven. The best strategy is to do what Venezuelan women do: ignore them completely, and keep walking.

When it comes to dating, the rules are fairly straightforward. Just as in dancing salsa or merengue, the man leads and the woman follows. This means that a woman will drop hints, laugh at lame jokes, and flirt with a man she fancies, but will wait for him to make the first move. For men from the USA or northern Europe, where it has become more typical for women to set the speed in relationships, taking the lead can sometimes be uncomfortable, but that's the way it works.

The other convention that should not be ignored is that if you invite someone out, you pay. There's no going Dutch in Venezuela. If a man were to suggest splitting the bill at a restaurant with a woman, or to buy himself a cinema ticket and expect her to buy her own, it would probably be the last date.

Typical first dates will be to a restaurant, the cinema, even an afternoon at a shopping mall for an ice cream and window-shopping. Venezuelan girls will often bring a cousin or friend along with them on these first dates to keep them company. It might take several dates before you get past holding hands. It's all part of the rather lengthy courting process in Venezuela.

Basically, the rules of the game are that a man will treat his girlfriend or wife like a princess, and pay for everything. Women will make an extra effort to make their man feel special by dressing up and taking care of their appearance, and being affectionate and attentive. It's an old-fashioned formula, but despite all the advances that women have made in education and the workplace, it doesn't show any signs of changing.

The End of the Fairy-Tale Romance?

There's a saying among men in Venezuela that women are sweet for as long as it takes to get what they want, and then they turn into a *cuaima*— a bushmaster (*Lachesis muta*), one of the deadliest snakes in the world. This idea of the nagging wife as the *cuaima* is found all over Venezuela, and is a popular stereotype in jokes and comedy shows.

I first came face to face with a *cuaima* at the top of the Ávila Mountain. Actors dressed as fairy-tale characters were posing for photos with children and their families. I asked a woman dressed in a green scaly costume whom she represented, and she laughed. "Enjoy yourself now, *muchacho*, because I'm your wife in two years' time. *La cuaima*. Your worst nightmare." She was the most popular character on the mountain that day.

HOMOSEXUALITY IN A MACHO SOCIETY

There is still a stigma attached to homosexuality in Venezuela, despite improvements to the legislation on equality. Same-sex civil unions are not yet legal, although there is considerable pressure on the government by the gay, lesbian, bisexual, transsexual, and transgender (GLBT) community to bring Venezuela in line with other countries in Latin America. In the meantime, conservative priests in the Catholic Church continue to preach that homosexuality is a sin, and the term *marico*— a slang word for gay—is often used as an insult.

The practical reality is that men who hold hands or kiss in public may find themselves stared at or perhaps the object of unkind comments or jokes, but there is rarely violence. It is probably better to follow the local code of conduct and restrict public displays of affection to places where there is a more enlightened audience, such as *bars de ambiente* (gay bars) or the beach resorts on Margarita Island or Choroni that are more laid-back about sexual orientation.

In Caracas and the other big cities there is a large, welcoming, and vibrant—if underground— gay scene, and making friends and filling your social calendar is easy. A good place to start is online. There are several Web sites that list gay-friendly clubs and restaurants (such as www.orbitagay.com), and Facebook lists a number of groups, including a "Venezuela GLBT" page with more than six hundred members.

One unmissable event for anybody interested in supporting gay rights in Venezuela is the annual Gay Pride March, held every July 4 in Caracas. It started in the year 2000 with just a few hundred marchers, and has grown to several thousand, including participation by politicians.

TIME OUT

Venezuelans have to work hard, but they also like to play hard, and take advantage of every opportunity to spend time with family and friends. Social and gregarious by nature, they prefer to spend their free time together, and the hot climate means that the parks are always full on weekends with children's parties and picnics and the beaches packed whenever there's a long weekend. Food plays a big part in social life, and everyone is a master at setting up a barbecue in an instant, or putting a big pot on to boil for a fish or chicken soup. For those days when there's nothing better to do, they're happy to head off to a shopping mall and spend the day window-shopping, snacking, and people watching.

VENEZUELAN FOOD

Venezuelans make the most of the tropical fruits and vegetables available to them, the grass-fed beef of Los Llanos, and the tasty tropical fish and seafood from the Caribbean. Food is also a reflection of the country's history, combining gastronomic elements from the indigenous inhabitants, the flavors of Spain and Africa brought over during colonial times, and the more recent tastes of Italy brought by immigrants after the Second Word War.

Arepas

The most distinctive local dish is the *arepa,* a corn-dough disk that is baked or fried, opened up like a pocket, and filled with grated cheese or other ingredients. Until the 1960s the process of shucking the corn kernels, grinding the corn by hand in a wooden *pilon,* and then preparing the dough made it difficult to mass-produce *arepas,* which were mainly consumed in the home. The arrival of precooked *harina* (flour) in 1960, however, sparked a boom in *areperas* (*arepa* bars) offering a large selection of fillings (see page 105). These are popular breakfast and lunch spots, and also get busy late at night with clubbers looking for a snack to soak up the booze.

Cachapas

Just as popular are *cachapas*. These are pancakes made from ground and grated corn, cooked on a flat griddle, and served with a slather of margarine and a slice of *queso de mano*, a soft white cheese .

They are often sold in the street, and are a staple at the Creole-style restaurants that serve *pabellon criollo* (see page 103) and *arepas*.

Fish
Along the coast and in the main cities, there is a large choice of Caribbean fish such as *pargo* (red snapper), *mero* (grouper), and *carite* (kingfish), usually served with *tostones* (fried plantains), rice, and a simple salad of grated carrot and tomatoes. The Andean state of Mérida has excellent *trucha* (trout).

Barbecue
Restaurants playing music from Los Llanos—with an obligatory cows' head on the wall for that rustic feel—specialize in *parilla* (barbecued food), serving up large steaks, chicken, *chorizo* (sausages), and *morcilla* (black pudding) with side orders of fried *yuca* (cassava). *Carne en vara* is beef cooked on a stick over an open fire. Try the *guasacaca*, a runnier version of Mexico's famous guacamole sauce, made with avocado, parsley, coriander, and bell pepper.

Soups
Mondongo (cow tripe and heel soup) is filled with thick root vegetables like *ñame* (yam) and *ocumo* (taro), and is believed to work miracles on a hangover. Other hearty soups are *auyama*

(pumpkin), *lenteja* (lentil), and *sancocho*, a combination of cassava, plantain, potatoes, corn cobs, peppers, and coriander boiled up with chicken, beef, or fish. *Cruzao* is a *sancocho* with two or more meats.

Empanadas

In most towns and cities you will find street stands selling *empanadas* (fried corn-dough turnovers) filled with cheese, beef, or chicken. *Empanadas* of *cazón (*baby shark) are popular at the beach. These are excellent snacks to stave off hunger between meals.

Bakery Snacks

The local *panadería* (bakery) is useful for much more than bread. It's the best place to get your coffee in the morning, and they serve juices and snacks like savory *pastelitos (*pastry turnovers filled with meat or cheese), *cachitos* (soft pastry half-moons filled with chopped ham and served hot or cold), sandwiches, sweet pastries, and *golfeados* (cakes).

Desserts

Venezuelans have a sweet tooth and enjoy desserts like *quesillo* (crème caramel), *torta de jojoto* (corn cake), the sticky *dulce de lechoza* (green papaya boiled up with brown sugar) and *dulce de guayaba* (sticky guava), and *bienmesabe* (sponge cake soaked in liquor and topped with coconut cream).

Regional Specialties

The emblematic dish of the Andes is *Pisca Andina,* a soup made with potatoes, milk, and coriander. Trout is another local staple, with trout farms producing a ready supply of this delicious freshwater fish. Andean *arepas* are made from wheat flour rather than corn.

In the arid deserts of Lara State, goats are the only livestock that prosper, and *chivo al coco* (goat in coconut) is a regional delicacy. In Zulia they prefer *conejo en coco* (rabbit in coconut), and prepare iguana in a similar manner.

Lau-lau (catfish) is fished from the Rio Orinoco and served up all year-round in Ciudad Bolívar, while another local fish, the *sapoara,* is eaten only in August at a festival in its honor.

In Amazonas State, indigenous tribes make a spicy sauce from ants called *katara,* which is eaten with *casabe* (flat disks of cassava bread). In the Gran Sabana, indigenous people from the Pémon tribe make a similar sauce but add termites for a crunchier texture.

The small mountain town of Colonia Tovar, a few hours' drive from Caracas, continues traditions brought by nineteenth-century German settlers from the Black Forest. Weekenders now make the drive to the high, cool valley to enjoy plates of pork knuckles, bratwurst, and sauerkraut, finishing off with locally grown strawberries and cream.

Flagship Food

Pabellon criollo is, without doubt, Venezuela's national dish. The name means "Creole flag" because of the colors of the ingredients, although for some it represents the mixture of races that has made Venezuela a country of beauty queens. The main ingredients are *carne mechada* (shredded beef), *arroz blanco* (white rice), *caraotas negras* (black beans) and *tajadas* (fried plantains). It is generally served with a few *arepas,* a slice of avocado, and salty white cheese grated over the black beans. If you order it *a caballo* (on horseback), it comes with a fried egg on top. Along the coast and on the island of Margarita the shredded beef is often replaced with *cazón (*baby shark).

The most exotic version of the *pabellon* is served during the Catholic fasting period of Lent when you may find *chiguire* (capybara) meat instead of beef. For some reason in colonial times the Catholic Church classified this giant rodent from the Llanos as a fish. Odd, but true!

TIPPING

Venezuelans will not leave a generous tip unless they feel the service they have received is particularly good, but will generally leave a few coins from the change or a BsF 20 bill rather than nothing. Generally, the more expensive and fancy the restaurant, the more likely a Venezuelan is to tip. There is no set amount or percentage for tips, and a 10 percent service charge is already included in the bill in restaurants. If you do receive good service and you want the waiter to remember you next time, tip 5 to 10 percent of the bill.

In hotels it is customary to tip porters the equivalent of a few US dollars. Tour guides should generally receive a tip, especially in remote areas where locals receive very little in the way of remuneration for their work. Tipping them is a good way to inject money directly into poor areas and show the benefits of tourism.

It is not typical to tip taxi drivers, but if you have hired a driver for a few days you may want to reward him with a small token of your appreciation.

EATING OUT

Most Venezuelans can only afford to eat out on paydays, which are every two weeks, so restaurants can get very busy on a payday Friday. For those with money in Caracas, there are a great many chic restaurants to choose from, options ranging from French, Italian, Thai, Peruvian, and Japanese, to

ORDERING AREPAS

Aguacate – Avocado

Aguita 'e Sapo (lit. "Frog Water" – don't let the name put you off) – roast pork in its juice, served with fried cheese. Found almost exclusively in Maracaibo

Caraotas negras – Black beans

Carne mechada – Shredded beef

Chicharrón – Fried pork rinds

Chorizo – Spicy sausage

Diablitos – Deviled ham

Domino – Black beans and grated white cheese

Ensalada de Gallina – Chicken salad

Montaña Rusa (lit. Russian Mountain, a roller-coaster ride) – Quail's eggs in mayonnaise

Morcilla – Black pudding

Orejas de Cochino – Pigs' ears in sauce

Pata-pata – Beans, yellow cheese, avocado

Pelua – Shredded beef, grated yellow cheese

Perico – Scrambled eggs, chopped tomato, onion

Pernil – Roast pork

Pollo guisado – Chicken cooked in a sauce

Queso de mano – Soft white country cheese

Queso Guayanes – Soft white cheese

Reina Pepiada – Chicken, avocado, mayonnaise, and peas

Sifrina – A *Reina Pepiada* with grated yellow cheese

every form of fusion food you can imagine. The main areas for elegant dining in Caracas are in Altamira and La Castellana, but Las Mercedes has many good restaurants and the upscale shopping malls in big towns and cities all have a variety of restaurants, bars, and nightclubs.

For those with less cash there are the usual food franchises like McDonald's and other US restaurant chains, as well as pizza parlors, restaurants specializing in spit-roasted chickens, Arabic places, Spanish tascas, and *parilla* places selling Creole food.

There is no culinary experience more Venezuelan than eating *arepa*s at an *arepera*, especially if you drizzle them with *guasacaca* (avocado sauce) and *picante* (hot sauce). You can go for a simple filling such as *jamon* (ham) or *queso* (cheese), but for the more ambitious there is plenty of variety.

DRINKS

One benefit of being in the tropics is the abundance of exotic fruits available. Freshly squeezed juices of *naranja* (orange) are called *jugos*, and juices made with water and liquidized fruit are called *batidos*. Typical flavors available at restaurants include *lechosa* (papaya), *parchita* (passion fruit), *patilla* (watermelon), *piña* (pineapple), *fresa* (strawberry), mango, and the *tres-en-uno* (three in one), a healthy combination of carrot, orange juice, and *remolacha* (beetroot). These can be very sweet, as sugar is added with the ice before liquidizing, so ask for a "*batido sin azúcar*" if you don't want to blow all your cash on dental bills. Milkshakes made with fresh fruit are called *merengadas*.

Fruit drinks sold in cartons in supermarkets and bakeries are heavily sweetened, as are chocolate milk drinks and the local *chicha*, a mix of milk and rice.

Water is not safe to drink from the tap, so you can drink filtered water, which some restaurants provide, or buy bottles, which are available from bakeries, supermarkets, and corner shops.

Alcohol

Venezuelans are big beer consumers, earning a well-deserved reputation as the Irish of South America. An ice-cold *cerveza* is seen as the best way to chill out after a hard day at work, and a range of lagers can be bought at liquor stores, supermarkets, and little hole-in-the-wall corner shops in poor neighborhoods. The leading beer company is Polar, a family firm that enjoyed a virtual monopoly of beer sales until the 1990s. Their polar bear brand is everywhere, and top sellers include Polar Ice, Polar Light, and Solera. Posters for the beer usually feature bikini-clad lovelies sipping a cold brew. Other beers are Brahma, Regional, and Zulia, and all are good-quality Pilsner lagers. You seldom find foreign beers in liquor stores, but some international hotel chains stock them.

Also good quality and good value are Venezuela's superb rums. They have to be aged for four years before they can be sold as rum, so even cheaper brands will taste good and be great for making cocktails. Top brands include Cacique, Santa Teresa, Diplomatico, and Pampero. Specially prized are Pampero Aniversario, which comes in a leather pouch, and Santa Teresa 1796.

Surprisingly, Venezuelans prefer whiskey to rum, and at one time were drinking more whiskey per capita than the Japanese. Don't buy a Venezuelan friend a cheap bottle of whiskey, or even an excellent

HOW DO YOU LIKE YOUR COFFEE?

Venezuela produces excellent Arabica coffee beans, and Venezuelans love to have morning coffee at a *panadería* (bakery) or café. Equipped with Gaggia machines, *panaderías* serve up coffee in two sizes: *café grande* (large) and *café pequeño* (small), equivalent to an espresso.

- A *café negro grande* (large black) is strong enough to give you the caffeine shakes.
- The oddly named *guayoyo* is black coffee that has been slightly watered down.
- For coffee with milk order a *con leche grande*.
- If you want an extra-milky coffee order a *tetero grande* (a *tetero* is a baby's bottle).
- For strong coffee with less milk ask for a *marron grande* or an even stronger *marron oscuro grande*. To make it extra strong, add the word *fuerte* at the end of your order.
- A *marron claro grande*, which some Venezuelans order, is basically a *con leche grande* by another name.
- For coffee with an extra kick order a *carajillo*, black with a shot of brandy, or a *café bautizado,* laced with rum.

single malt, as they favor Johnnie Walker Black Label and Chivas Regal over other brands. One unusual Venezuelan habit you might notice is the popularity of drinking whiskey at the beach mixed with ice and coconut water.

Wine doesn't have much of a market outside the main cities, and most Venezuelans will use cheap Spanish table wine for cooking rather than drinking. The only local wine producer is Bodegas Pomar, a subsidiary of Polar, which produces a very decent range from its vineyards in Carora, Lara State.

Another local brew is the supersweet cocktail of passion-fruit juice, sugar, and *aguardiente* (raw cane alcohol) called *guarapita*. Sold at beach resorts like Choroni and Chuao along the central coast, it is guaranteed to get you in the mood for dancing to the local Afro-Venezuelan *tambores* (drums).

NIGHTLIFE

Venezuelans have a reputation for being party people. They love to dance, at home with friends or out at bars and nightclubs.

With street crime an issue nowadays, many Venezuelans will go to bars and clubs in the large shopping malls, where they feel safer, but in poorer areas, where everybody knows their neighbors, you will still find people sitting outside their houses drinking and chatting or going from house to house to hang out with friends.

There are plenty of options to choose from if you want a night out in the big cities. Caracas has a host of nightspots for every pocket, from sweaty salsa clubs like El Mani Es Así to chic joints playing electronica. The Centro San Ignacio shopping mall in La Castellana is where you find the smart set, and prices to match, at laid-back joints like Sukabar. The 360 Rooftop Bar on the nineteenth floor of the Altamira Suites is a popular spot for sipping mojitos and enjoying panoramic views over the city, and the nearby Ávila Lounge Bar in the Pestana Hotel offers similarly chic surroundings.

You don't have to wear a suit and tie at these places—smart casual will generally do—but the dress code in Caracas is quite conservative, and people are turned away from some of the smart clubs, bars, and restaurants if the doorman considers they are not appropriately dressed.

Caracas also has a vibrant live music scene, with rock and indie acts playing clubs like Teatro Bar and the tiny Puto Bar and jazz acts playing the Juan Sebastian Bar, which is a veritable institution.

The university city of Mérida, with its large student population, also has great nightlife, with a circuit of cheap bars playing music in the center and shiny discos in modern shopping malls.

SPORTS

Venezuela's sports are dominated by *beisbol*, which was brought to the country by US engineers working in the oil camps in the 1950s and adopted as a local religion. Games between the top rival teams, Los Leones de Caracas, and Los Navegantes del Magallanes, are major events, with fans so loyal that it can cause divisions in families. When the Caracas and Magallanes meet, the atmosphere at the stadium is like a huge party, with men and women dressed in their team colors quaffing beer and cheering wildly throughout the game.

Everything stops for a major baseball game. President Chávez, a huge baseball fan and a promising player in his youth, would never interrupt a game with one of his marathon speeches. He once joked that supporters of his team, Magallanes, would make good wives, because they stay loyal.

Many Venezuelan players have gone on to play Major League Baseball in the USA, including Luis Aparicio, Omar Vizquel, Andrés Galarraga, and Johan Santana. The Washington Nationals catcher Wilson Ramos made international headlines for all the wrong reasons in November 2011, when he was kidnapped near his home in Valencia, Venezuela, and held for two days before being rescued. The incident highlighted the country's serious crime problem.

Compared to other South American nations, football (soccer) is nowhere near as popular as baseball and basketball, but it is rapidly building a following and the national team La Vinotinto (The Burgundy) have beaten some top regional teams in recent qualifiers. Venezuela has never played at the World Cup, but the dream is getting closer.

CINEMA

Most large shopping malls have multiplex cinemas that show all the latest Hollywood movies with subtitles in Spanish. Art house movies are shown at specialist cinemas like the Transnocho in Las Mercedes, Caracas.

A recent initiative to boost local movie production, La Villa de Cine, has sponsored several historic dramas about independence heroes and the acclaimed *Postales de Leningrado*, a magical realist tale of a group of guerrillas in the 1960s, directed by Mariana Rondon. The biggest movie to come out of Venezuela in recent years is *Secuestro Express*, directed by Jonathan Jakubowicz. The Tarantino-style black comedy stars Edgar Ramirez, a Venezuelan actor who has had international success in *The Bourne Ultimatum* and starred as Carlos the Jackal in a French film about the Venezuelan terrorist's turbulent life.

The most famous Venezuelan actress in Hollywood is the ex-supermodel Patricia Velásquez, who comes from Zulia and has Wayuu indigenous roots. She had a starring role in *The Mummy* movies, appeared in the US TV *Ugly Betty* series, and recently starred in *Cenizas Eternas* (Eternal Ashes), a film about the Yanomami Indians.

The most popular movie to feature Venezuela as a backdrop is the Oscar-winning Pixar-Disney cartoon *Up!* about a grumpy old man who travels to Roraima and Angel Falls in a house carried aloft by balloons.

THE ARTS

Caracas has a number of very good private art galleries and museums, including the Museo de Bellas Artes, the Galería de Arte Nacional, and the Contemporary Arts Museum, which owns works by international artists such as Picasso, Miró, and Botero.

The most famous modern Venezuelan painter is Armando Reverón (1889–1954), who lived as a Robinson Crusoe hermit with his maid Juanita in a stone and bamboo house he built himself near Macuto. Reverón tried to capture the blinding tropical light of the coast in expressionist works painted in shades of white.

Other artists include the nineteenth-century master Arturo Michelena (1863–98), who painted an iconic image of independence hero Francisco de Miranda languishing in a Spanish jail. Modern artists of note include kinetic artist Jesús Rafael Soto (1923–2005), who has a museum of his work in Ciudad Bolívar, and his contemporary Carlos Cruz-Diez (1923–), whose monumental kinetic works are found on the Caracas Metro.

Theater, ballet, and opera companies put on well-attended shows at the very modern Teresa Carreño cultural center in Caracas, and an International Theater Festival in April–May brings international groups to enrich the city's rich cultural life.

MUSIC

Venezuela throbs with music, and everywhere you go you hear salsa, merengue, and reggaeton. The most surprising musical phenomenon in the country, however, is the profusion of classical orchestras and the quality of music being played.

There are thirty-plus symphony orchestras and more than 125 youth orchestras in Venezuela, all thanks to a foundation started in 1975 by economist José Antonio Abreu called El Sistema, which teaches music to some 250,000 children, the vast majority of them from the poorest homes. The biggest star to

emerge from El Sistema is the conductor Gustavo Dudamel. He started his career with the Simón Bolívar Youth Orchestra and has become one of the hottest properties in classical music, constantly shuttling between Sweden and the USA as lead conductor of the Gothenberg Symphony Orchestra and musical director of the Los Angeles Philharmonic.

Salsa star Oscar D'Leon, the Lion King of salsa, is another homegrown hero who constantly tours the world. Other musical talents are the Latin Grammy-winning tropical-pop-rock group Los Amigos Invisibles, veteran ska group Desorden Publico, and upcoming art rock band La Vida Boheme.

SHOPPING FOR PLEASURE

Dressing up in new clothes, wearing designer labels, and having the latest gadgets are all part of the Venezuelan lifestyle, and shiny shopping malls have sprung up to cater to every need in Barquisimeto, Mérida, Maracaibo, and Porlamar on Margarita.

The Sambil shopping mall in Caracas is one of the largest in South America, housing more than five hundred shops, banks, and pharmacies. People spend the whole day there, shopping, window-shopping, getting their hair cut, and showing off their new outfits. For kids, there is an aquarium and fun park; for adults there are fast-food outlets, cinemas, and bars. With virtually everything imported, prices are generally higher than in the USA.

Foreigners looking for souvenirs in Caracas should head to Hannsi in El Hatillo, a treasure trove of folk art from around the country. Coffee beans, sipping rums, and indigenous handicrafts also make great gifts.

In rural areas, head for the colorful street markets that sell local goods and regional foods. In Puerto Ayacucho the indigenous market sells beads made from jungle seeds, bows and arrows, and spicy sauces made from termites and ants.

With Caribbean beaches just an hour away from Caracas, it's tempting to adopt a Florida-style approach in the street and wear shorts, but it's worth noting that this is not considered appropriate attire for entering banks and other offices, and you could be barred entry by the security guard—a time-consuming delay that is best avoided.

TOP VISITOR ATTRACTIONS

Venezuela is so vast and has so many spectacular tourist spots that it is impossible to see them all in a short visit. Here are a few must-see attractions.

Angel Falls

The most iconic natural wonder of Venezuela is the highest waterfall in the world, Salto Ángel (Angel

Falls), a single cascade of water that plunges 3,212 feet (979 m) down a sheer rock face. The base of the falls can be reached only by dugout canoe from the landing strip at Canaima, which has helped to preserve the pristine forests surrounding it.

Margarita

Margarita Island is a typical Caribbean resort destination, with a different beach to visit each day, clubs, casinos, and world-class windsurfing at El Yaque.

Los Llanos

Bird-watchers head to the seasonally flooded cattle plains of Los Llanos to see waders and birds of prey, but are equally impressed by herds of capybara and rivers teeming with snappy piranhas and caimans.

Mérida

The Andean valleys around Mérida make for great hiking, but you can also paraglide, mountain bike, and go white-water rafting as the area earns a name as the adventure sports capital of Venezuela. Rising high above the city are the craggy peaks of the Sierra Nevada and Venezuela's highest point, Pico Bolívar, at 16,342 ft (4981 m). It has the world's highest cable car, which is currently undergoing a major refurbishment but is expected to be operating again soon.

Caracas
The artistic and cultural capital of Venezuela has plenty to offer in terms of sophisticated nights out, great restaurants, interesting museums, and historic monuments. Fear of crime limits visitors to the safer east of the city.

Los Roques Archipelago
Just forty minutes in a light aircraft from Maiquetia airport is this Caribbean paradise of tiny coral sand islands surrounded by warm, crystalline waters. Honeymooners bask in the waters and relax, families

snorkel, adrenaline junkies dive or kitesurf, while sport fisherman fly in from around the world to enjoy first-class bonefishing.

Mount Roraima

Hikers can't get enough of the six-day trek from Santa Elena to the summit of Roraima, the mountain that inspired Sir Arthur Conan Doyle to write his adventure book *The Lost World*. The highest of the towering *tepuis* (table mountains) that make the topography of the Gran Sabana region so memorable, Roraima is an eerie place of labyrinths of ancient sandstone, carnivorous plants, and hopless prehistoric toads.

chapter **seven**

TRAVEL, HEALTH, AND SAFETY

GETTING AROUND

Venezuela has a good transportation infrastructure, with flights linking all the major cities and most tourist destinations, an extensive system of asphalted highways crisscrossing the country, and an efficient subway system in Caracas. Access to cheap petroleum has historically favored roads over rail, and it is only now that the government has started to invest in railroad construction, principally by extending the Caracas subway system to the suburbs and nearby satellite towns.

As elsewhere in the tropics, health care and precautions are an important consideration. Travel insurance is essential, and should cover everything you do during your stay, including adventure sports if you plan to windsurf, paraglide, or go white-water rafting. You should also ensure you get all the necessary inoculations before you travel. Prevention is better than cure.

An increasingly challenging crime and safety situation over recent years has meant that visitors should be extra cautious about when and where they travel in Venezuela, but by following sensible advice it is still possible to enjoy the magnificent natural beauty of the country, as the top tourist destinations are generally much safer than the cities.

Venezuelans carry their ID card, known as a Cédula de Identidad, with them at all times. This is because they can be stopped at a police or National Guard checkpoint, and anybody without a valid ID can be detained until they can prove their identity. Foreigners are not exempt from these rules, and are advised to carry their passport with them at all times. Photocopies of ID documents are not generally accepted, even from tourists. It can be unnerving to be woken on a long-distance bus by armed men in uniform, but the best approach is to remain calm and, of course, polite. They are only doing their job, and it doesn't help to annoy them.

BY AIR

Apart from the odd charter flying in to Margarita, most international flights arrive and depart from the Simón Bolívar international airport at Maiquetia, about an hour's drive from Caracas. Airports in the USA with direct flights to Venezuela are Miami, Atlanta, Houston, Los Angeles, and Dallas. Flights from the main European hubs, except for those from

the UK, are direct. From Maiquetia airport there are domestic flights to all major cities.

High inflation has made domestic air travel more expensive than it was a few years ago, but of course it is the quickest way to commute the vast distances between some cities and to reach holiday hot spots such as Margarita, Mérida, and the Gran Sabana.

New airlines have recently entered the market, and others have expanded their routes. The main airlines include Avior, Aserca, and the state-owned airline Conviasa. Aerotuy has small planes operating the route to Los Roques and other remote tourist destinations and Transmandu flies small Cessnas that link Ciudad Bolívar and Puerto Ordaz to Canaima, the jungle base for trips to Angel Falls.

ON THE ROAD
City Buses

In Caracas there are modern Metrobuses that link the subway system to other parts of the city. They are clean, efficient, have bus stops, and run more or less to a timetable.

For most journeys Venezuelans rely on the hundreds of owner-operated *por puestos* buses, sometimes called *camionetas* (minivans) that clog the streets of Caracas and other cities and towns. These have their destinations on the front windshield, and you simply wave your arm to flag one down. Usually, the driver has an assistant who collects the fares as passengers get on, and shouts out the destination. There are no set stops for *por puestos*, and they add to the general chaos by constantly speeding up and slowing down, cutting in front of each other to beat their rivals to potential passengers, and stopping in the middle of the road to let people off. *Por puesto* travel is usually accompanied by tropical tunes like salsa, merengue, or headache-inducing reggaeton. To cut through the noise of the sound system, passengers clap their hands to ask the driver to stop, or shout "*En la parada, por favor*" ("Stop here, please").

At the main bus terminals in some towns you find *carritos*, or *carritos por puestos*, which are cars that operate as a bus service, charging by the seat and only setting off when full. Routes generally have set fares, and if you're in a hurry you can pay for all the empty seats and set off straight away.

Long-Distance Buses

Internal flights are out of the budget range of most Venezuelans, who are more likely to travel the long distances between cities by bus. Most journeys start from the main *terminal de pasajeros* (central bus station) of each town or city or from the depots of private bus companies. Service is frequent, and many long-distance buses travel at night.

The main terminal in Caracas is a three-story bus station called La Bandera, a chaotic crush of humanity as people try to buy tickets at the jumble of bus company offices on the upper floor. It is almost impossible to buy bus tickets online or in advance on these buses, so the only way is to turn up on the day of travel and get what you can. At holiday times the crowds at La Bandera can swell to massive proportions, so plan to leave a few days before the rush and return a few days after the main holiday dates if you are taking a bus during these periods.

Cold Toes and Video Nasties

Expect Arctic conditions on long-distance buses. For some reason the companies insist on keeping the air-conditioning on full blast for the whole journey. Venezuelans are used to this, and will take woolly hats, sweaters, coats, and blankets. I once traveled to Puerto Ayacucho in Amazonas State, and dressed for an expedition up the Orinoco in long shorts and a T-shirt. Five minutes into the twenty-hour journey I realized that I was severely underdressed and would freeze if I didn't take action. Seeing my predicament, a Venezuelan woman across the aisle invited me to share her duvet, and I was saved. Now I wear long trousers and pack a fleece and blanket when traveling.

The other problem on buses is the videos they play. On a twenty-three-hour bus trip from Santa Elena to Caracas, after six exhausting days climbing to the top of Mount Roraima, all I wanted to do was curl up and sleep. Instead, I was treated to five films featuring Jean-Claude Van Damme, played back to back and with the sound at a level that made dozing off near impossible. I just remember one film blurring into the next as I slipped in and out of sleep, promising myself that next time I'd bring some earplugs.

At other, smaller bus terminals it is easier to get tickets on the day of travel, but the only companies that allow you to book online or in advance are the ones with their own terminals, such as Aeroexpresos Ejecutivos (www.aeroexpresos.com.ve).

Buses have varying grades of comfort, and prices to match. An Expreso just means a fast intercity service. Ejecutivo implies a greater degree of comfort on board, and a Bus Cama (Bed Bus) will have seats and footrests that allow you to recline. On the twelve-hour journey between Caracas and Mérida, a Bus Cama taken at night allows you to sleep.

Taxis

There are several types of taxi operating in Venezuela. There are those that work in *lineas de taxi* (taxi stands) at airports, hotels, and shopping malls, with their company logo clearly visible; there are dial-up taxi companies that will pick up you up wherever you are; and there is the type known as a *libre* that drives around waiting to be flagged down.

All licensed taxis have special yellow number plates, and are typically white with a yellow and black checkered band—although the official taxis at Maiquetia airport are black Ford Explorers. Unlicensed taxis, known as *piratas* (pirates), will sometimes put a plastic taxi sign on the roof when looking for fares, but should be avoided, even if they do offer cheaper rates.

Always agree on the fare before getting into a taxi or booking one on the telephone, as they don't have meters. You don't normally tip for a routine trip.

In some places it works out more cheaply to use taxis and buses to get around than renting a car, and you don't have to worry about finding a safe parking space. If you are going out at night in the major cities, always take a taxi, as walking is not recommended after dark.

If you are hiring a taxi for several days, try to negotiate a day rate for the whole car, not per passenger, and make sure you specify the places you want to visit, and the start and finish times each day, to avoid arguments. Pay at the end of a journey, not up front, and then, if you feel you have received good service, a tip would be in order.

Mototaxis

If you don't mind taking a risk and really need to get somewhere fast during rush hour, then you might feel like jumping on the pillion of one of the thousands of motorbike taxis, or *mototaxis,* that buzz around Caracas like so many busy bees. By weaving through gridlocked traffic, mounting the sidewalk, and ignoring the rules of the road, *mototaxis* can greatly reduce travel times in a city overrun by cars and buses. Riding scooters or motorbikes, *mototaxistas* work out of cooperatives based on busy corners. A report in 2011 estimated that some eight hundred cooperatives were operating in Caracas, ferrying ordinary people to poor slums where buses don't run, or rushing businessmen across the city to important meetings. Although passengers are provided with a helmet, the dangers of riding on a *mototaxi* are many, as accidents are frequent and the bikes themselves can be the targets of armed thieves.

Car Rental

Taxis and buses are probably the cheapest way to travel. However, if you plan to spend a few days exploring somewhere like Margarita Island, with gas prices so low it might be worth renting a car for the convenience.

International car rental firms including Hertz, Avis, and Budget operate at most airports, and cars can be ordered from abroad online. To rent a car in Venezuela, you will be required to take out insurance, pay with a credit card, and be over twenty-one. To rent a four-by-four vehicle, around double the cost of a small car, you will need to be over twenty-five.

Always check the tires, brakes, and seat belts, and note any dents with the rental agency before taking the car. In Venezuela a car must by law be equipped with a reflector triangle in case of accident. Ensure you have all the tools and security devices noted down correctly.

Driving Rules

Venezuelans drive on the right, as they do in the USA, but the driving experience is quite different and the rules of the road are rarely respected. Particularly in Caracas, drivers swerve about and cut in front of each other, pass on either side, and honk their horns for no obvious reason, and the chunkiest, most aggressively driven vehicle wins. Add in the *por puestos*, which stop and start to pick up and let off passengers, and the *mototaxis* and motorbike couriers weaving in and out, and you have a recipe for chaos.

Drivers are supposed to wear their seat belts. Checks are made at roadside checkpoints set up by the police and National Guard.

There is a speed limit of 40 kmh (25 mph) in cities and 80 kmh (50 mph) on main roads, but it is virtually unheard of for anybody to be charged with breaking the speed limit.

Running red lights is endemic, especially at night, and there are no effective deterrents to drunk driving, as Breathalyzers are seldom if ever used. The only way to survive is to drive defensively at all times.

However, if you are stopped at a police checkpoint, or are involved in an accident and the transportation police are called, you will find yourself in trouble if you do not have all the necessary documents for yourself and the car.

Gasoline
With the cheapest gas prices in the world, it's no wonder that Venezuelans with cars drive everywhere. Gas costs about 2 US cents a liter (about 8 cents a gallon) and filling your tank is cheaper than buying a liter bottle of water. All gas stations sell unleaded gas, such as 89 or 95 octane, and in cities there are plenty of gas stations. If you are travelling to the rural areas, however, it is better to fill up in advance. In some border areas, such as Santa Elena, on the border with Brazil, there is rationing to stop Brazilians from exploiting the price difference at the pumps and effectively smuggling gas over the border to sell. This can result in long lines at gas stations.

TRAINS
The Subway System
The Caracas Metro is fast, efficient, and (outside rush hours) a great way to get around the city. Opened in 1983, with just one line running from Propatria in the west to Palo Verde in the east, the Metro has now expanded to three lines. From Parque Central Metro station there is a link to the Metrocable, a small-scale

cable car system that serves the hillside *barrios*, which started limited operations in 2009.

More extensions are planned, and the system is gradually linking central Caracas with the major suburbs outside the valley. One of the new lines will link up the Metro to the Warairarepano cable car station at Mariperez, which takes passengers to the top of the Ávila Mountain.

As *por puesto* prices have risen in Caracas, Metro fares have stayed relatively low, due to subsidies, and the government has made travel free for those over the age of sixty-five. The result has been a dramatic increase in passenger numbers, to the point at peak hours when people have to cram themselves forcefully into the cars. This can be hot and uncomfortable, can result in altercations between passengers, and makes the work of pickpockets easier.

Both Maracaibo and Valencia have inaugurated their own Metro systems, which have started to operate limited services.

The Railway System

Up until the 1950s, when the decision was made by the dictator Marcos Pérez Jimenez to undertake an ambitious building program of new highways and other projects, including the two massive concrete viaducts on the road to the airport, Venezuela did have some railways. The Puerto Cabello to Barquisimeto train is a relic of the days when Caracas was linked to Valencia and La Guaira by rail.

Now Venezuela is again turning to railways, with plans to build new lines at several points around the country. The first of these was completed in 2006, with an electric line from La Rinconada Metro in Caracas to Charallave and Cúa in the Tuy Valley. Built by an Italian, French, and Venezuelan consortium, the 25 miles (40 km) of track cost US$1.9 billion and has twenty-three tunnels, one of which is 4.2 miles (6.8 km) long. The trains travel at a swift 75 mph (120 kmh). A second stage will link Puerto Cabello to Cagua.

FERRIES

The main links to the tourist island of Margarita are the car ferry from Puerto la Cruz and the fast passenger ferries from Puerto La Cruz and Cumaná. A small car ferry also operates between Margarita and the tiny island of Coche.

The biggest line is Conferry (www.conferry.com), which was taken over in 2011 by the government, with frequent delays and poor operating standards cited as the reason. The other ferry company is Naviarca-Gran Cacique (www.grancacique.com.ve).

WHERE TO STAY

Venezuela has all the usual accommodation options, ranging from five-star luxury hotels in the major cities to hammocks strung up under the stars in jungle camps. It is worth noting that prices tend to rise during high season (*temporada alta*), which includes Christmas, New Year, Carnival, Easter, and the school breaks in July and August.

Caracas is the most expensive place to stay, given its importance to business travelers, and there is a choice of international chain hotels with all the modern conveniences, swimming pools, and Wi-Fi. Smaller boutique hotels have also started to spring up in larger cities. Margarita, which is a magnet for

Venezuelan vacationers during holiday periods and long weekends, also has a range of high-end hotels and beach resorts, many offering package deals. In hotels, a *habitación doble* can mean twin beds, while a *matrimonial* is a room with a double bed.

The greatest concentration of accommodation options on the mainland is in Mérida State, with more than 140 small hotels and 170 *posadas* (guesthouses), including the basic but lovely *mucuposadas*—rustic family homes in the high Andean valleys around the city of Mérida that have been converted to offer rooms and meals to hikers. *Posadas* are found in the countryside and along the

coast, and can be quaint colonial houses or modern concrete blocks. These family-run establishments usually have fewer rooms and can be more rustic than small hotels, but on Los Roques, where there are strict building regulations, the Italian-owned *posadas* are decorated in a grand Mediterranean style, and have prices to match.

In Los Llanos, some large cattle ranches, called *hatos*, offer accommodation to wildlife enthusiasts and bird-watchers. Hato el Cedral in Apure State is one of the most famous of these. Accommodation is basic but comfortable, and there is a small pool.

Be aware that some of the motel-like places seen along major highways and on the outskirts of towns, especially the ones with romantic-sounding names, are "love hotels," known in Venezuela as *hoteles de cita* (date hotels) or, more crudely, as *mataderos* (slaughterhouses). Equipped with mirrored ceilings and Jacuzzis, and as busy at lunchtime as they are at night, these discreet establishments don't cater solely to unfaithful spouses. Many people use them because they can't afford to move out of the family home, and have nowhere else to be with their partners. Extra discreet versions, for those who really don't want to be seen, have two-story units with a parking space below and a garage door that lowers to hide the car.

HEALTH

The public health system in Venezuela is free to all, but is hampered by a lack of organization and supplies. The conditions in some public hospitals are very primitive, and the system often depends on family members to provide medicines and food for patients, and in some cases to supply basics like bandages and gauze.

A world apart from the public health system, there is a thriving private health care sector offering sophisticated scans and lab tests, emergency facilities, plastic surgery, and all major operations for those who can afford to pay. Medical staff are well qualified in the private sector, and treatment is good, but as in the USA and other countries private health care is not cheap, and must be paid for up front, or at least before patients are discharged. Foreigners with insurance will still need to pay by cash or a credit card before being admitted for treatment, as most insurance companies pay out only on your return.

For minor ailments, many people head first to a *farmacia* and ask the pharmacist for advice. Some medicines and antibiotics that would need a prescription in the USA or northern Europe are available over the counter. If it's late, and the local pharmacy is closed, it will display a list of nearby pharmacies that are open.

Venezuelans who can't afford private doctors or who live far from public hospitals often go to the small clinics set up in poor areas run by Cuban doctors, part of an oil-for-doctors deal between Venezuela and Cuba known as Misión Barrio Adentro (Inside the Barrio Mission). Attempts to expand this parallel health care system have hit snags as the main federation of Venezuelan doctors has challenged the legal rights of Cuban doctors to practice medicine in Venezuela.

Precautions
Venezuela is a tropical country close to the equator, and visitors are advised to take basic precautions when spending time in the sun. Always wear sunscreen with a high protection factor, and reapply it regularly after swimming. Drink plenty of liquids, and wear a hat to avoid sunstroke.

Tap water is not safe to drink, but can be used for cleaning teeth. Many restaurants and *posadas* offer filtered tap water, which is fine, but if you're not sure ask for bottled water.

Traveler's diarrhea is a possibility, so pack Imodium, Kaopectate, or a similar product, which will help when traveling on flights or long bus journeys. Usually, this clears up on its own and is just a reaction to a change in routine, new foods, and hot weather. Rehydration salts will also help.

Before traveling to Venezuela you should make sure to have the required immunizations. A tetanus-diphtheria booster shot is recommended if you haven't had one in the last ten years. Typhoid, hepatitis A, and hepatitis B immunization is recommended. A yellow fever shot is not compulsory, but is needed if you expect to cross into Brazil by land, in which case bring the certificate, as you will be required to show it.

Some parts of Venezuela, including the more remote areas of the Orinoco Delta, Bolívar State, and Amazonas, carry a risk of malaria and other insect-borne diseases. Consult a medical professional for the latest advice before taking antimalarial medication. In rural and coastal areas, use insect repellent, wear long sleeves and long pants after sunset, and sleep under a mosquito net.

SAFETY

Crime levels have increased markedly in recent years, and Venezuelans list crime and insecurity as their chief concern. Business travelers and tourists are advised to exercise all sensible precautions, particularly while in Caracas and other cities, and should heed the advice of their embassy, which will have advice on security issues on its Web site. The city of Mérida, while not completely crime free, is seen as a safer alternative to Caracas for tourists wanting a base from which to explore Los Llanos and other destinations.

The constant fear of crime in Caracas is reflected in the barred windows and security doors on houses and apartments, and the armed security guards outside supermarkets and gated communities. This is partly due to the general rise in drug-related crime throughout Latin America, but is also down to poor policing, collusion between police officers and criminals, and corruption in the judicial system, which allows those who can pay to avoid justice. The understandable paranoia is fueled by newspaper and TV reports filled with frightening stories of murders, muggings, and "express kidnappings" (*secuestro express*), in which victims are taken to ATMs or banks and forced to empty their accounts over a short period of time before being released.

Along with an increase in robberies and kidnappings across the country, Caracas has earned a reputation as the murder capital of the world. The weekend murder rate regularly tops fifty murders, with most taking place in poor hillside *barrios*, where life is cheap and drugs are rife.

Other hot spots are located along the border with Colombia in Tachira, Zulia, and Apure States, since guerrillas, paramilitaries, and organized crime gangs have carried out kidnappings in those regions.

A report by the Observatorio Venezolano de Violencia (Venezuela Violence Observatory), a local NGO, stated that according to the crime figures collated in 2011 by university researchers the murder rate could be as high as 19,336—or 67 murders per 100,000 inhabitants—a national record.

STAYING SAFE

- Don't attract the attention of thieves. Leave gold chains, good jewelry, and expensive watches at home and keep digital cameras and cell phones out of sight.
- Don't change money in the street. Try to use hotels or travel agents for changing money, and avoid street hustlers, who will offer a higher rate just to see, and then steal, your cash.
- Safety in numbers. Solo travelers, especially women, can be targeted.
- Learn some Spanish. The more you can speak and understand, the better.
- Listen to local advice on places to avoid, and don't enter shantytowns.
- Know where you are going. Don't wander around with a map, looking lost. Take taxis at night.
- Avoid crowds. Don't travel on the subway or buses during peak hours because pickpockets, including minors, will be taking advantage of the crush.
- Use the hotel safe. Don't walk around with all your cash, but always have something on you to hand over if mugged.
- If you do get held up, hand over your stuff. Keep calm, and don't resist.
- Have a backup. Keep emergency bills hidden under your clothes or belt, or in your shoes, just in case.
- Copy documents. Scan your passport, airline ticket, and other documents, and e-mail yourself a copy.

chapter eight

BUSINESS BRIEFING

If you do your homework, make the right contacts, and find people to help you cut through the red tape and advise you on the legal regulations, Venezuela is a dynamic market in which to do business. As elsewhere in South America, who you know is as important as what you have to sell, and putting the time into networking and face-to-face contact will be crucial to the success of any business venture you embark upon.

There are three expressions that sum up the business experience in Venezuela. *Buena gente* means "good people"—essentially, people you can trust. It's important that you are seen as *buena gente* and that you know how to recognize others. A *palanca* is a lever, but in business terms it means somebody who is on the inside, or is close to people on the inside, who can arrange for you to have a meeting with decision makers or other important people in an organization, or can get things moving if they stall. Finally, a *gestor* is a fixer, or middleman, who can steer you through the paperwork needed to make a business work, take care of imports and exports, cut down the time it takes to set up bank accounts, and organize currency exchange.

Depending on the kind of business you plan to do, you'll also need legal advice from a recognized in-country expert. You will also need patience and flexibility, because finding the people you need, organizing meetings, and dealing with unforeseen delays and setbacks can be a long and sometimes frustrating process.

THE BUSINESS LANDSCAPE

The effects of strict currency controls, price fixing, tougher import and export controls, and high inflation have all added to a more challenging business environment over the last few years, a fact reflected in the World Bank's 2012 Ease of Doing Business ranking, which placed Venezuela 177th out of 183 countries, below Zimbabwe, Haiti, and Guinea-Bissau. That said, Venezuela is still a vibrant market with many opportunities in the oil and gas sectors, food franchises, and high-end consumer goods. Venezuelans are born entrepreneurs, and

continue to be avid consumers of branded goods and the latest gadgets.

PERSONAL RELATIONSHIPS

Dressing right, making a good impression, networking, and spending the time to get to know the right people are all very important in Venezuela. Generally, Venezuelans are risk averse and like to operate in an environment where they know who they are dealing with. This is where the concept of *buena gente* comes in. If a potential business partner or customer believes you are a good person to do business with, then you have a better chance of sealing a deal. But getting to know people takes time, and foreign businesspeople eager to get things moving in Venezuela are often frustrated when initial meetings seem to revolve around social pleasantries rather than getting straight down to business. This is normal. Once a good relationship has been established, things will start to move, but perhaps not as fast as they would in the USA or Europe. This is where networking comes in. The key is to meet people who can help you meet other people and get you direct contact with the company chiefs and decision makers whom you would have difficulty in contacting yourself.

Dress Code

Although Venezuela is a tropical country, formal business dress is expected at meetings and business-related social events. Men typically wear dark business suits and ties, and it

is not considered appropriate to arrive wearing a tie without a jacket. Most offices have air-conditioning, but it's acceptable to remove your jacket once seated. Businesswomen typically wear a smart dress, or skirt or trousers with a neat blouse, and look well groomed.

You should also dress smartly when meeting a potential client for a meal or drinks. Venezuelans set great store by what you wear, and are not impressed by jeans and T-shirts.

USEFUL ORGANIZATIONS

Seeking to do business in Venezuela, foreign companies that don't have the advantage of good personal contacts should approach established business associations, which can provide information on the business climate and markets, and steer you toward reliable local partners and reputable legal firms. These include the Venamcham (Cámara Venezolano Americana de Comercio e Industria/ Venezuelan American Chamber of Commerce and Industry) and the Venezuelan British Chamber of Commerce (Cámara Venezolano Británica de Comercio). The trade representative of your country's embassy in Caracas can also help with contacts and local advice. Venezuelan bodies such as CONAPRI (Consejo Nacional de Promoción de Inversiones/Venezuelan Council for Investment Promotion) can also be useful.

WOMEN IN BUSINESS

With 52 percent of university enrollment held by women and a strong representation in accountancy, marketing, law, medicine, engineering, and management courses, you are as likely in Venezuela to find yourself doing business with a woman as with a man. Natural entrepreneurs in a society where you have to work hard to make ends meet, women have traditionally been the backbone of the economy. It is not unusual for women to take on two jobs to get their children through school, and in most offices there will be at least somebody with a sideline in cosmetics, dietary supplements, clothes, or kitchenware to supplement their monthly salary.

Businesswomen in Venezuela are respected professionals, and visiting businesswomen are treated with the same respect. When meeting a woman in a business environment, shake hands when introducing yourself, as you would with a man. A kiss on the cheek would be seen as unprofessional.

ARRANGING A MEETING

When dealing with government bodies, the process of making appointments is formal, bureaucratic, and sometimes very slow. It is best to start at your local Venezuelan embassy, unless you have a direct contact, and begin with a formal letter and e-mail in Spanish. If you can get a trade attaché or ambassador to recommend you as somebody personally known to them, things will move faster. If you have a *palanca* in Venezuela, even better, as they will be able to get you into the office where you can arrange a meeting in person.

With large businesses used to dealing with foreign companies a direct e-mail in Spanish is

acceptable for proposing dates for a meeting, but it should be followed up with a phone call about two weeks before the meeting and another the day before just to check that everything is on schedule. This might seem like overkill to foreign entrepreneurs, but in Venezuela, where things can change quite quickly and where businesspeople are juggling many things at the same time, you need to keep in touch, gently remind people you're coming, and use the opportunity to build a rapport.

Entrepreneurs who have spent months sending out e-mails from their home country without any concrete leads will find that once they are in Venezuela they will start to see results. This is because Venezuelans prefer to deal with people face-to-face, and once they know you personally will be more likely to introduce you to other business acquaintances and help set up meetings.

Sometimes, when dealing with smaller companies, the e-mail correspondence might seem vague, and you might be asked to "pass by the office when you are in Venezuela" rather than being given a set time for an appointment. Basically, you have to come to Venezuela and meet people in person if you want results, and part of the challenge, as in most places, is understanding who has the power to do business with you and sign off on deals and how you can get hold of them.

TIMING OF MEETINGS

An important consideration when scheduling appointments is that Venezuelans take their weekends and public holidays seriously, and there is little chance of getting anything done on a Friday afternoon or during the long holiday periods around Christmas/New Year, or Carnival/Easter.

The best time for a meeting is in the morning. Depending on the size of the company, you may be invited to a brunch meeting with several executives and decision makers where you can discuss things over coffee and a pastry. These often act as premeetings and a chance to find out more about you. Don't be frustrated if you don't get down to business right away. This is not the place to get a decision. The same holds true for lunch meetings. Be aware that an invitation to dinner is probably down to a hospitable concern at the thought of your being alone in an unknown city rather than a burning desire to do business with you there and then. The key thing to remember is to remain professional at all times, even when out on the town, and that the etiquette in Venezuela is for the person making the invitation to pay the bill. Never offer to pay half the bill, as it will look cheap. Offer to pay it all, but don't insist, as this may cause offense. It's better to let your host pay and for you to invite them for the next meal.

PUNCTUALITY

The vagaries of traffic, tropical downpours, and a laid-back attitude to timekeeping by some Venezuelans can all result in a late start. A foreign businessperson should arrive on time, however, although not before, and to do so will need to factor in potential transportation delays. If you do have to wait, even for an hour or so, or even reschedule the meeting for another day, this is nothing personal; it's just a local peculiarity that you will have to get used to. The important thing is not to get ruffled or show undue annoyance by last-minute changes, and to make sure you leave room in your schedule for contingencies.

MEETINGS AND PRESENTATIONS

The formalities of a meeting usually begin with a greeting to the group of "*Buenos días*" or "*Buenas tardes*," depending on the time of day. Then you will be presented to each person in the room. It is typical to shake hands and say, "*Mucho gusto*" (Pleased to meet you) or "*Un placer*" (It's a pleasure).

Bring business cards written in English on one side and Spanish on the other. Any material or brochures you bring with you should also be translated into Spanish, preferably by a local translator to get the tone right and avoid words with different meanings in different Spanish-speaking countries.

Presentations should also be given in Spanish. Unless your Spanish is very good, you will need an interpreter or intermediary/partner who can translate, even if some people in the room speak English. Generally, senior executives in large private companies will speak English, but you can't guarantee this, and anyone attending the meeting because they have key expertise pertaining to the deal may understand no English at all. When dealing with government agencies you should always bring a translator and have a document drawn up in Spanish with the main points of your proposal.

Questions may be asked in a very direct way, but don't take this as confrontational. Give calm, measured responses. The key here is to keep your cool and remain friendly and professional. Don't be put off if there is conversation during your presentation, or if people take phone calls or leave the room while you are speaking. This is just another example of a more relaxed attitude to doing business.

NEGOTIATIONS

Having given your pitch and answered questions, don't expect an immediate answer. Several other meetings may be needed before a deal is finalized. Very often you will be told that somebody else has to be consulted, and when dealing with government agencies that is probably the case, but in private firms this could also be a polite way of saying, "We'll think about it and get back to you."

If negotiations drag on too long, however, it probably means that the Venezuelan business is avoiding a straight "no" in favor of subtle hints. Having local contacts more used to the subtleties of Venezuelan negotiations will help to interpret the responses you receive.

CONTRACTS AND LEGAL CONSIDERATIONS

Unlike the legal systems in the USA and UK, which rely on judicial precedents, Venezuela has a "written code" or "civil law" legal system, like the ones in France and Spain. The laws are a combination of the national constitution, legal codes, laws laid down in federal, state, and municipal entities, and presidential decrees.

Under the national constitution the government has the right to own certain industries that are considered "strategic," including those related to the oil and gas industry and the generation and distribution of electricity. Other sectors considered strategic by the present government are telecommunications, the production and distribution of food, and heavy industries.

With such a complicated and wide-ranging legal landscape it is advisable to seek guidance from a well-respected law firm on all the legal issues pertaining to any potential business venture before going ahead. Use a local lawyer and professional translator to draft contracts in Spanish and English, and clarify any contractual issues before signing on the dotted line.

MANAGEMENT STYLE

In a Venezuelan business environment the hierarchy of a company is very important, and people treasure their titles. It is typical for an engineer to be addressed as "Ingeniero" or a university graduate as "Licenciado" in the same way as a US employee would address a superior as "Sir." Foreign entrepreneurs would not be expected to use such titles when addressing people, but should be aware of them and should use *usted* (the formal singular form of "you") when speaking to senior executives.

A foreign businessperson managing Venezuelan staff would be expected to act as a boss and maintain a certain distance with staff while at the same time exhibiting enough empathy for them to be able to express their concerns.

GIFT GIVING

You are not expected to bring gifts when doing business, but as so much business depends on personal interaction and keeping relationships friendly then it is not uncommon, after the first visit, to bring something

from your home country on subsequent visits. Given the universal appeal of Scotch whiskey, a bottle of Black Label or Chivas Regal will generally be appreciated.

When dealing with government agencies, however, especially if bidding for contracts, it is considered best practice to avoid giving expensive gifts as this can give the wrong impression.

DEALING WITH RED TAPE

Doing business in Venezuela has become increasingly tied up in red tape as a result of changes to import/export rules, currency and price controls, and greater tax and labor regulations. A trip to the bank to make a simple transaction can take up to half a day, and visits to government offices to present paperwork can be equally frustrating. Using a reputable *gestor* to help deal with the more onerous elements of red tape can greatly cut down on the time involved, and for importing or exporting goods through customs this is essential.

chapter **nine**

COMMUNICATING

LANGUAGE

The official language of Venezuela is Spanish, and almost everybody speaks it as their first language apart from the indigenous groups, who are generally bilingual. People will often say that they speak *castellano* (Castilian Spanish), and technically they do, but the Venezuelan accent is softer than the Spanish spoken on the Spanish mainland and closer to the accent of the Canary Islands. One of the first things you will notice is that Venezuelans do not have the characteristic lisp on the "*c*" and "*z*" that you hear in Spain; *cerveza* is pronounced "sirvesa." Another characteristic is that some people swallow the last consonant on words and leave out the "*s*" when speaking fast, so the word *pescado* (fish), for example, sounds like *pecao*.

When speaking in formal situations—to elders, teachers, bank clerks, superiors at work, and especially the police or National Guard—Venezuelans will use the formal singular pronoun *usted* (you), but they will quickly slip into the informal *tu* once a closer bond has been established. It is always better to use *usted* on first meeting a person, especially if you want to build a professional relationship with them, as it shows respect and good manners, and this will be noticed. Venezuelans use *ustedes* for both the formal and informal second-person plural, rather than *vosotros*, which is used in some other Latin American countries.

REGIONAL DIFFERENCES

The accent used in Caracas, known as Caraqueño, is considered the standard Venezuelan accent, but there are many regional differences. The people of the Andean states of Mérida and Táchira, which border Colombia, are known as Gochos, and have a reputation for speaking slowly and having good grammar. The inhabitants of Los Llanos, known as Llaneros, have a nasal delivery with a slight lisp, and Margariteños, from the tourist island of Margarita, speak very fast. The people of Lara State are known as Guaros, for their use of the term "*na' guara*" meaning "no way!" or "wow!" to indicate disbelief or surprise. The biggest difference in speech is found in Zulia, where the local form of Spanish, called Maracucho or Marabino, is named after the inhabitants of Maracaibo. Maracuchos use the archaic second person pronoun *vos* (you) instead of the more typical *tú*, with the verb endings -*eis*, -*ais*, and -*is*, rather than -*as* and -*es*. This differs from the *vos* forms used in other parts of Latin America and is a source of pride to the regionalist Maracuchos.

SPANGLISH

Many years of US involvement in the oil industry, the influence of US TV programs, and Venezuelan travel to the USA are reflected in the amount of Spanglish spoken in the country. At a gas station, Venezuelans will tell the attendant they want their tank "*full de gasoline*," and after a meal it's typical for somebody to say "*estoy full*" (I'm full). Other Spanglish words are *fútbol (soccer)* and most words related to the national sport *béisbol*, such as *jonrón* (home run). A security guard at an office or supermarket is a *guachiman*, a plumber is a *plomero,* a winch is a *guinche*, and the verb *tipiar* means to type. Less obvious is the very popular word *macundales,* which means gear, things, or stuff. It comes from the Mac and Dale tools that the oil workers were given by the American oil companies. Wherever they went they had to take their tools with them, and the expression "*llevate tus macundales, nos vamos*" ("get your stuff, we're leaving") was born.

SPEAKING SPANISH

English is studied as a second language by almost every schoolkid in Venezuela, but few people can speak it. In beach and country areas you are unlikely to be met with anything more than the basics of "How are you?" and "What is your name?"

The more Spanish you can learn before you go, the better. You will be able to ask for things and understand the replies, and you will find it easier to make meaningful contact with the people you meet. Once you are in Venezuela, any attempt to speak Spanish will be met with appreciation, especially if you can use some basic Venezuelan expressions. A simple "*chévere!*"— meaning "cool!" or "great!"—delivered with a smile, will be sure to endear you to your hosts.

VENEZOLANISMOS

Speaking a few words of Venezuelan Spanish is the best way to show Venezuelans an interest and respect for their country and a desire to communicate. It's also an excellent icebreaker, and is generally greeted with a smile. Venezuelan Spanish evolved in the melting pot of the Spanish conquest, when Iberian settlers mixed with indigenous tribes and the African slaves brought to work the sugar and cacao plantations. More recent additions include the oil camp Spanglish, brought by US engineers, and Portuguese and Italian phrases brought by the immigrants after the Second World War.

Chamo/chama Boy/girl

Chévere! Cool, great, nice, wonderful. A very useful word. Some people will tell you that it comes from the American Chevrolet car, but it's actually from Africa and the Yoruba expression "*ché egberi*."

Chimbo/chimba Bad, rotten, uncool, fake

Épale Hey! A typical conversation starter, or a way to get somebody's attention

Jeva Girlfriend

Ladilla Literally, crab louse. A dull or annoying person or situation

Mira Look! A typical conversation starter or a way to get somebody's attention

Pana Buddy, friend. "*Hola, pana*" (Hey, buddy) is a typical greeting, even between strangers.

Sifrino/Sifrina Snob, posh

Zanahoria Literally, carrot. Healthy. Someone who eats well and exercises.

Those planning to stay longer in the country can find good schools teaching Spanish to foreigners in Caracas, Mérida, and Margarita Island.

OTHER LANGUAGES

There are some twenty-eight indigenous languages spoken in Venezuela. The most populous indigenous group is the Wayúu (also known as Guajiros), who number about 300,000. Their native territory in the desert region around the Guajira Peninsula covers both sides of the border with Colombia, and there is a large Wayúu community in the city of Maracaibo. Other large groups are the Warao of the Orinoco River Delta (36,000) and the Pémon (28,000) of the Gran Sabana area bordering Brazil. The Yanomami are the most famous and most studied indigenous tribe and about 15,000 Yanomami live in the remote forests of the Orinoco region bordering Brazil.

ETIQUETTE

In a country where personal contacts are important, people take meeting and greeting seriously. Men will shake hands with all the other men in a group, introduce themselves, and say "*Mucho gusto*" (Pleased to meet you) or "*Un placer*" (It's a pleasure). Male friends are less formal and will sometimes backslap and bear hug even recent acquaintances, which can take some foreign visitors by surprise. When meeting women, the etiquette is for one kiss on the right cheek—except in a business situation, where a handshake is correct.

Venezuelans can be very familiar or very curt with strangers, especially in shops and restaurants, where service sometimes verges on chummy pestering or complete indifference.

However, people are very aware of good manners, and when entering a room Venezuelans will normally say to those present "*Buenos días*" or "*Buenas tardes,*" depending on the time of day. Also, in restaurants or at dinner it is customary to say "*Buen provecho*" (Enjoy your meal) to other diners.

Elderly people are treated with respect and referred to as *Señor/Señora* or *Don/Doña*. It is usual for a younger person to give up their seat for an elderly person on the bus or subway.

Cover Up!

One thing that surprises some visitors, given the figure-hugging clothes worn by many women in the street and the tiny thongs they wear at the beach, is the conservative attitude to topless bathing. On a popular beach on Margarita Island I once witnessed an outraged young mother call a policeman on to the beach to insist that a pair of German tourists put their bikini tops on. The poor girls could see nothing wrong with what they were doing, but the tut-tutting crowd of Venezuelan women who quickly gathered around them made it clear that they thought going topless in front of children was beyond the pale. The apologetic young police officer told the girls that personally he was quite happy for them to continue as they were, but that going topless was technically illegal and they would have to cover up.

HUMOR

Venezuela is a macho country, and comedy shows are firmly stuck in the Benny Hill era, with voluptuous girls in bikinis and curvy maids with feather dusters fighting off the advances of eager older men. Sketch shows rely on stereotypes for laughs, with the Gallego, or Spaniard, as the butt of many jokes. Another source of humor is the macho man in the bar whose wife has him under her thumb at home.

Venezuelans love a laugh when gathered with friends, generally at the expense of somebody in the group. This is known as *chalaqueo*. Don't worry if you get a gentle ribbing; it's all part of the game. People are used to facing adversity and will readily share a joke about the chaos of the Caracas traffic, the long lines in banks, and the other frustrations of the day.

Angry Wife Gets Even

There was a man who was proud of his wife for having had six children. Rather than use her name he would always call her "Mother of Six." This really upset the wife, however. One day at a wedding, in front of the whole family, he shouted across the room, "Are you ready to leave, Mother of Six?" She shouted back, "Any time you want, Father of Five!"

Dead Funny

A grieving widow at the funeral parlor hears a knocking and a voice from the coffin. "Open up! They're going to bury me alive." "Quiet, Paco, you always think you know better than the doctor!"
(*Provided by Venezuelan comedian Emilio Lovera*)

BODY LANGUAGE

Nonverbal communication is a big part of
Venezuelan life, and foreigners will find people to
be more tactile and touchy-feely than is usual in the
USA or the UK, and more energetic in their use of
gestures. Examples of this are the kiss when greeting
women and the backslap between men. One of the
oddest gestures is the habit of indicating where things
are by puckering up the lips and pointing with them.
You'll see this used in shops, and when giving
directions. It could be partly explained by the laziness
brought on by working in a hot climate, but it is so
ingrained that you'll find it almost everywhere.
Another typical gesture is the crinkling up of the
nose, like a rabbit, when somebody doesn't
understand what you've said.

In restaurants you'll hear people using a hissing
noise to get the waiter's attention. This is not
considered rude. You'll also see people catch the
waiter's eye and write an imaginary check on the
palm of their hand, to ask for the bill.

Tapping the elbow indicates that someone is
stingy with money. Pulling down the lower eyelid
with the forefinger is a warning sign and is usually
accompanied with the word *mosca* (literally, fly),
which means "be careful," or "danger!" When
indicating approval, use your raised thumbs rather
than an "O" formed with the thumb and forefinger,
which is very similar to a Venezuelan gesture
meaning "gay."

Another peculiarity is the applause that breaks out
among Venezuelan passengers when a plane lands.
Feel free to join in.

THE MEDIA

Since President Chávez came to power in 1999 there has been increasing polarization and politicization of the Venezuelan media, with the main newspapers and TV channels taking a strong line against the government and the few state-supported media outlets carrying the government line. The president has characterized the situation as a war against his socialist revolution by a few powerful media owners, while the opposition media have characterized the situation as an attack on press freedom by an autocratic government. One result of this was a law, passed in 2005, that increased the penalties for libel and defamation and made it a criminal offense to show disrespect to the president. While the opposition press has labeled it a "gag law," it has not muzzled the press, but it has resulted in a measure of self-censorship.

Newspapers

The most respected national newspapers are the broadsheets *El Nacional* and *El Universal*, which have

taken a strong line against the government of President Chávez, and the tabloid *Ultimas Noticias*, which has taken a more middle-of-the-road approach to politics and seen its readership increase. The most politically hostile newspaper is *Tal Cual*, which often features front-page articles critical of the government.

Television

Television has been a constant in the lives of most Venezuelans since a government drive in the 1950s under the dictator Marcos Pérez Jiménez sought to get a TV set in every household. Around 75 percent of programming is provided by broadcast television, and cable and satellite TV provide the rest. The four biggest private networks are Radio Caracas Televisión (RCTV), Venevision, Televen, and the twenty-four-hour news channel Globovision. The oldest channel, RCTV, was forced to become a satellite and cable service in 2007 after the government refused to renew its broadcasting license, blaming it for supporting the 2002 coup that briefly removed President Chávez. The move sparked accusations of a crackdown on freedom of expression.

State-owned TV channels include Venezolana de Televisión, Tves, and Vive TV. Their share of the audience is minimal. The Venezuelan government was also behind the launch of TeleSur, a pan-Latin-American satellite and cable channel that began broadcasting in 2005. Cosponsored by the governments of Argentina, Bolivia, Cuba, Ecuador, Nicaragua, and Uruguay, TeleSur has a marked left-leaning political agenda.

Perhaps the most distinctive feature of Venezuelan TV is the regular *cadenas* (literally, chains)—interventions on all TV and radio channels by President Chávez whenever he wants to speak to the nation. These interventions can sometimes go on for hours and infuriate soap opera fans if they interrupt a cliff-hanger moment, but the media-savvy president is clever enough not to interrupt an important baseball game. A regular *cadena* that Venezuelans can prepare for is Chávez's Sunday program *Aló, Presidente*, on which he lauds the advances of the Bolivarian revolutionary project, harangues the opposition, tells jokes and stories about his life, and even breaks into song.

Radio

The radio plays a big part in the life of Venezuelans, whether it's the mainstream news and music stations such as FM Center—the largest AM and FM radio network and the main provider of traffic updates in Caracas—or traditional news stations like Radio Rumbos. There is a host of local community stations, many sponsored by government grants. The law states that radio stations must dedicate a certain percentage of their output to locally produced content, and must play one Venezuelan song for every foreign one, in a bid to stimulate the local music industry.

INTERNET

Venezuela is a highly connected country, and has the third-largest Internet usage in Latin America, after Argentina and Chile. For many Venezuelans, the

Internet is starting to take over from TV as their main source of information. A report in 2011 estimated there were more than 10 million Internet users—nearly 40 percent of the population. The largest provider of home broadband is the state telecoms company CANTV, while 3G mobile broadband coverage, which has been slower to develop, is led by Movistar and Digitel.

The millions of Venezuelans who still have no mobile broadband or home access continue to use cyber cafés, which are easily found in large cities and small towns and offer cheap Internet connection. Most hotels and many small *posadas* geared for foreign tourists also have Wi-Fi, usually offered free to guests.

In the student city of Mérida, a popular destination for foreign tourists, Internet access is so widespread that it is said to have more computer users per capita than Tokyo.

Another development is a system of government-run Infocentros in cultural centers such as libraries and museums. These centers are free to use and are equipped with computers with high-speed Internet access, color printers, and scanners. The government plans to extend this network to remote indigenous communities, such as the Pémon village in Canaima.

Venezuelans on the Net
Just as Venezuelans love to hang out and socialize in real life, they are also avid users of social networking sites. About 86 percent of local Internet users have a Facebook account, and the use of Twitter has also boomed in recent years, especially among politicians. Seeing a great opportunity to get his point across,

President Chávez caused a Twitter sensation when he opened his @chavezcandanga account in April 2010. He signed up 95,000 followers in the first thirty-six hours, and by December 2012 had 2,461,250 followers. He reportedly needs twenty assistants to cope with the hundreds of messages he receives each day from critics, supporters, and people asking for jobs, houses, and help with health issues.

TELEPHONE

The sole provider of fixed landlines is the state-run telephone company CANTV, which was renationalized by President Chávez in 2007. CANTV also operates *Centros de Comunicación* (call centers), where you can make local and international phone calls and use the Internet. Given the long waiting lists  and red tape associated with installing a landline, Venezuelans have adopted cell phones in a big way. Land coverage is close to 99.2 percent, with more than 28.9 million mobile phones in use in 2009. The three main cell phone providers are Movistar, owned by Spanish firm Telefonica (0414 and 0424 numbers), Movilnet, owned by CANTV (0416 and 0426) and Digitel, owned by the Cisneros group (0412). Venezuelans are keen users of BlackBerrys, with more than a million users, but these are a top target for thieves. Many Venezuelans carry two or three phones to minimize the high cost of calls between providers. In most large and small towns, you will find street vendors renting out cell phones to make short calls.

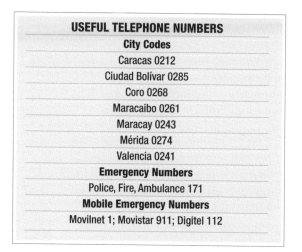

USEFUL TELEPHONE NUMBERS
City Codes
Caracas 0212
Ciudad Bolívar 0285
Coro 0268
Maracaibo 0261
Maracay 0243
Mérida 0274
Valencia 0241
Emergency Numbers
Police, Fire, Ambulance 171
Mobile Emergency Numbers
Movilnet 1; Movistar 911; Digitel 112

MAIL

The national postal system, Ipostel (Instituto Postal Telegráfico), is notoriously slow. Letters can take two weeks or more to arrive at their destination. Stamps and postcards can be purchased at hotels, which saves a trip to the post office.

There is little point in sending a parcel to Venezuela from abroad through the postal system, as it can result in a frustrating experience for the recipient, who will have to travel to the central post office to collect it and may have to pay duty on the contents. More reliable are international courier companies, such as FedEx and DHL, which operate throughout Venezuela. The lack of an efficient postal system is the reason for the swarms of motorbike couriers, or *motorizados,* who zip around Caracas in the thousands, ignoring traffic lights and mounting sidewalks when it suits them.

CONCLUSION

Over the last ten years international news about Venezuela has been dominated by political events in the country, the extreme polarization between supporters of President Chávez and those who oppose his Bolivarian revolution, as well as the public spats between the Venezuelan government and the USA at international forums. While these developments are undoubtedly important to an understanding of Venezuela today, it would of course be blinkered to see the country only through this prism.

As we have seen, the people of Venezuela are optimistic and forward-looking, quick with a joke, and welcoming to strangers. We hope that, having learned something about their history and the cultural complexity of modern Venezuelan society, you will feel confident enough to venture out and explore this fascinating country with a better understanding of the people you'll meet along the way.

The future of Venezuela may be an open book—but, whatever happens, it will never be a dull one.

Further Reading

Blessed, Brian. *Quest for the Lost World*. London: Boxtree, 2000.

Brokken, Jan. *Jungle Rudy*. New York: Marion Boyars, 2004.

Chasteen, John Charles. *Americanos: Latin America's Struggle for Independence*. New York: Oxford University Press, 2008.

Conan Doyle, Sir Arthur. *The Lost World*. London: Vintage Books, 2011.

Gallegos, Romulo. *Doña Barbara: A Novel*. Chicago and London: University of Chicago Press, 2012.

García Marquez, Gabriel. *The General in his Labyrinth*. London: Penguin, 2008.

Gott, Richard. *Hugo Chávez and the Bolivarian Revolution in Venezuela*. New York: Verso, 2005.

Harvey, Robert. *Liberators: Latin America's Struggle for Independence*. Woodstock, New York: Overlook Press, 2000.

Hilty, Steven. *Guide to the Birds of Venezuela*. Princeton. Princeton University Press, 2003.

Hudson, W.H. *Green Mansions: A Romance of the Tropical Forest*. London: Gerald Duckworth, 2008.

Humboldt, Alexander von. *Personal Narrative of Travels to the Equinoctial Regions of America*. New York: Penguin, 1995.

Jones, Bart. *Hugo! The Hugo Chávez Story: From Mud Hut to Perpetual Revolution*. London: The Bodley Head, 2008.

Lynch, John. *Simón Bolívar: A Life*. New Haven: Yale University Press, 2007.

Maddicks, Russell. *Bradt Guide to Venezuela*. London: Bradt, 2010.

O'Hanlon, Redmond. *In Trouble Again: A Journey Between the Orinoco and the Amazon*. New York: Penguin, 1989.

Reid, Michael. *Forgotten Continent: The Battle for Latin America's Soul*. New Haven: Yale University Press, 2007.

Index

culture smart! venezuela